IN HIS HEALING STEPS

IN HIS HEALING STEPS

by
GEORGE BENNETT

Author of
Miracle at Crowhurst
The Heart of Healing

Published by
ARTHUR JAMES LIMITED
THE DRIFT, EVESHAM, WORCS.
WR11 4NW

First Edition 1976

ISBN 0 85305 188 7

SCRIPTURE SOURCES

Unless otherwise stated all Scripture quotations have been taken from the Authorised Version.

MADE AND PRINTED IN GREAT BRITAIN BY PURNELL AND SONS, LTD., PAULTON (AVON) AND LONDON

DEDICATION

to

JACK and JAN

FOREWORD
by
the Right Reverend Morris Maddocks, the Bishop of Selby

THESE ARE EXCITING DAYS for Christians. The good Lord seems to be renewing His church with spiritual gifts that alone will equip her "for work in His service" in tempestuous times. One of the fruits of Christ's bounty which is much in evidence again in this era of renewal is the charismata iamaton (gifts of healing—1 Corinthians 12:9).

The Holy Spirit is leading us back into the Truth of Christ's original commission to the Twelve—Preach *and Heal.* We must pray for a spirit of discipline and obedience to fulfil our discipleship, and for an outpouring of whatever "charismata" are necessary to make perfect the Lord's strength in our weakness.

George Bennett, for whom I am honoured to write this foreword and who needs no introduction from me, is one of Christ's servants who has been thus equipped and mightily used in recalling the church to her calling to heal. What blessings have followed his obedience to the call to go out with Abrahamic faith and follow the promptings of the Spirit in his (now) wider ministry—leading healing missions and clergy conventions in many parts of the world. Many, like myself and several of my colleagues in the York diocese, owe him a debt of gratitude for leading us to a fuller *awareness* of, and *obedience* to, Christ's call (two of George's great words). Many who read this book will praise the Lord for gifts of healing shown forth in themselves, their families, their congregations perhaps because George was used as a channel for the charismata. Christ the Healer wills to work through His obedient servants in His world today; "He has no other hands—but YOURS."

It is fitting that George Bennett has chosen the seventieth anniversary year of the Divine Healing Mission, of which he is President, to publish his latest book and so complete a trilogy on the subject of healing. His first book, *Miracle at Crowhurst,* a personal record of his eleven and a half years' ministry at this home of healing which was blessed and guided by God in so many ways, has become an encouragement to many in this field of ministry. *The Heart of Healing,* his second book, provided teaching and guidance to help recover this lost dimension of the church's ministry. In his foreword, the present Archbishop of Canterbury referred to "the strong pastoral sense by which it is marked throughout". George is a pastor indeed.

Now he gives us *In His Healing Steps,* a study of this ministry in greater depth, an essay in the theology of healing. I hope it will become required reading among all clergy and in theological colleges. Some of it is material he has used in speaking to such specialist audiences. But it will be helpful to all who seek the glory of Christ the Healer.

It is recorded that Pope John XXIII's addresses frequently had three ingredients: "an historical basis, a personal reminiscence and a cogent reference to the Gospel" (Meriol Trevor in *Pope John,* p. 205; Macmillan, 1967). George has a similar method: his theology here is Gospel-based and cogently expressed (there are several studies of Gospel healings), while the chapters are illustrated and illuminated by personal reminiscences and case histories. He also has a compelling philosophy of history, outlined in his great penultimate chapter, "A New Beginning", in which he has some constructive things to say about the charismatic movement and the more traditional and sacramentally-based ministry, which he sees as a "both—and" situation, not "either—or".

"Is this work of healing," he asks, "more evangelistic than pastoral in its nature?" A good question. The ever-increasing offering of expectant prayer by Christians all over the world is leading to signs following and opening many doors through which thousands are beginning to catch a glimpse of "His glory, full of grace and truth" for the first time.

My hope is that this book will be used by Christian groups for thought and study, because if it is read prayerfully I believe it will open a new dimension of faith. If we follow *In His Healing Steps* the healing Christ turns round at the moment of His choice to say, as He did to St. Andrew, "Come and see". This book is a veritable confrontation with Christ the Healer. The result may well be a new vision of the way in which He wishes His church to follow in those healing steps. I pray this new vision may be for you, your group, your church, your community and for the world He came to heal and save.

York 1976. + MORRIS SELBY

PREFACE

I SHOULD LIKE to thank so many friends, both in England and overseas, for the prayerful support and encouragement they have given me in the writing of this book. I hope they will feel it to be a worthwhile contribution to the current recovery by the church of her healing ministry. The substance of some of its chapters they will recognise as having already been presented in addresses given in various parts of the world. We live in exciting times when the Lord is re-fashioning His church into the body of His own indwelling through which He wants to work today as ever He did of old. And we rejoice as, following in His Healing Steps, we discover that His promises are as true for us today as ever they were for His first disciples.

I would also like to thank my publishers for the help they have given me and for their patience with me. Many have cause to thank God for their untiring dedication in the task to which God has called them, and I, for my part, deeply value their friendship, encouragement and advice.

I would like to express my gratitude to Mrs. Eileen Roberts for the part she has so readily played in preparing the final script.

And, finally, my thanks for more things than I can mention here go to Jack and Jan Head to whom this book is dedicated.

GEORGE BENNETT

CONTENTS

Page

Foreword by the Bishop of Selby vii
Co-Chairman of the Churches' Council for Health and Healing

Preface xi

Chapter

I Where Healing Begins 15

II In the Name of Jesus 25

III A Healing Atmosphere 33

IV The Springs of Healing 44

V The Works of God 55

VI The Captain of Our Salvation 60

VII A Faith Without Limit 72

VIII As a Grain of Mustard Seed 83

IX The Awakening of Faith 91

X The Spreading of Faith 103

XI A New Beginning 114

XII So Send I You 123

I

WHERE HEALING BEGINS

"FOR AS LONG as I remember," a lady said to me, "I have attended church regularly yet never once did it occur to me that I might look there for healing." She had suffered aches and pains in her back for many years and had at times found the effort of trying to walk almost too much for her. It was not until she attended a healing mission and received the touch of Christ through the laying-on-of-hands at the concluding service that the trouble left her.

The church she had been regularly attending had given her solace. There is no doubt about that. Her minister and some of the fellow-members of her congregation had been kindness itself. Their friendliness and encouragement had enabled her to become a shining witness to God's grace in the midst of her infirmity. No doubt she had become, though she did not say this, an example to others.

But now she was free! A wonderful thing had happened to her. At first, she could hardly believe it. In the days that followed the service she found she could move her limbs as she had not moved them for many years.

Some time later she told me, in a quiet moment of thanksgiving, there had been a time when she thought of turning for help to a faith healer. A member of her church had suggested this to her. Her minister, perhaps wisely, had dissuaded her when she asked him. But, perhaps not so wisely, he had really no alternative advice to give except that she accept her troubles "in the spirit of Christ" by thinking of them as being somehow bound up with the whole work of His redemption. This she had learned to do.

Her minister was, very happily, among the first to praise God for the new and wonderful thing that had happened to her. Throughout the mission his heart had been opening to a dimension of the gospel he had never experienced before. Finally, he had joined me, with a number of other clergy and ministers, in ministering the laying-on-of-hands in Christ's name to the many people who attended the service. This lady, helped to the communion rails by a couple of friends, had been among them.

It always seems strange to me, and the more so as I read the gospels, that even among Christians the work of healing is sometimes considered to be extraordinary.

A clergyman to whom I was recently introduced confessed, "I believe in healing, but I have my reservations." The last word sounded heavy and full of meaning! It was hardly the time for a lengthy discourse on what the word "healing" means, nor of the relationship between medical healing and what, for want of a better phrase, we sometimes call divine healing. Probably, if I had had the same ideas as he, I would have had my reservations, too!

The pity is that something which is simple at root has been made to look complicated; and what is natural to the gospel, unnatural. The result has been that what ought to be an essential ingredient in the experience of every Christian congregation is often regarded as something not to be looked for and, in some quarters, even contrary to the Gospel.

This negative attitude has largely been shaped by our instinctive reaction to the sensationalised press reports of healings performed by all kinds of queer people with strange ideas over the years. The image left in our minds has had a distorting effect on the real truth. To mention healing often raises this unfortunate image in our minds and it triggers off a reaction of mistrust and suspicion. The damage has been done. I can well understand this. Sometimes watching television or looking at the pictures in an illustrated magazine when the subject under discussion is healing we are presented with a demonstration conducted by somebody who is unlike other mortals. He, or she, is in touch with strange and unseen powers that are denied to ordinary folk.

Yet even here, amid the morass of oddities, I sometimes detect an element of the truth creeping in. At least they accept the fact that there is an unseen world about us that penetrates this one, that there are powers in the spiritual world which can have effective expression in ours.

It is easy enough for us to judge and to say these things are all wrong and that we want none of them, but we cannot free ourselves of all blame. For centuries we have largely ignored the second part of our Lord's twofold commission. We have been prepared to preach and to do plenty of that! But we have pushed the work of healing on one side. The result has been that man's inborn and instinctive search for healing on a deeper level than that provided by purely material means has led him to look elsewhere and he has produced substitutes. And those who have an inbuilt sensitivity to the realm of the unseen, and might well have been used in the service of the church, have turned aside.

We are now living in a new era when the Holy Spirit is making us realise once again that, despite our present divisions, we are called to be the body of Christ through which He wants to work today as ever He did. The hands that have for so long been tied are stretching forth again to bring healing to the sick. Often when I am speaking to large congregations at Teaching and Healing Missions I get the strong impression that they are recognising a message for which they have long been unconsciously seeking. There is a movement of deep apperception in the midst that could not have been experienced twenty or thirty years ago.

No doubt there is yet a long way to go. This new era is only at its beginning. We have much to learn—or, rather, re-learn about the laws of the spiritual realm that lie behind prayer and the work of healing. When I think about the fresh insights that the Holy Spirit is bringing into our consciousness again in these days it is as though we have had a door opened to us which leads into a large room full of beautiful things. At the moment we stand on its threshold while our souls and minds try to assimilate and make sense of what we have been shown so far. There is far more waiting to be unfolded to us, but as, in simple obedience to our Lord's whole command, we put our hands in His, we can be sure He will guide us safely through the jumble of strange and distorted ideas into the wonderful simplicity of it all.

For, basically, the reason why Jesus healed is very simple. He healed because it was of His nature to heal. One might say He healed because He couldn't help it.

That was the kind of person He was. And, because He is the same yesterday, today and forever, this is the kind of person He still is. Simply to be in His presence is healing.

I have from time to time come across simple folk who had been badly hurt by life and the purpose of my visit was to bring them help. But when I came away I knew it was I who had been helped, and that far more than they. Not that they knew what they were doing. The help they gave was unconscious on their part. They did not set out to be healers, yet the burdens I was carrying at the time grew lighter and easier simply because I had been for a while in their presence.

I once had an aunt like this. Though she was a skilled and highly qualified physiotherapist it was not so much of her treatments that her patients spoke but, rather, of her presence. With her calm and reassuring manner she always seemed to bring a spirit of peace and healing into their rooms as soon as she entered.

I remember having asked her if she ever felt a power other than her own flowing through her hands into the sick bodies of those she ministered to. "But of course!" she said. "And not only into their bodies!"

She was one who had an instinctive understanding of the ministry of healing. I could always talk easily with her in the days when I first began to give the laying-on-of-hands. She understood perfectly the strong impulsion I was feeling. Strangely, I find many of my doctor friends also have a deeper insight into this aspect of the church's ministry than do some of our clergy! Perhaps they know what a healing presence can mean. And what a touch can convey.

Godfrey Mowatt, who did so much in the early days

for what has now become the Churches' Council for Health and Healing, was one of those who had such a presence. He was a channel of God's healing to many, and not only because he ministered the Lord's touch through his hands. There was an atmosphere of heaven about him that even the most materially minded folk could sense. Just to sit quietly with him for a while, without necessarily a word being spoken, somehow brought healing and peace. Perhaps the fact that he was blind enabled him to "see" farther than most people can. And this brought him a deeper sensitivity than most ordinary people have.

I remember thus sitting with him many years ago when our children were young and we were finding it hard to make ends meet. It was in the entrance hall of the National Liberal Club, of which he was a member, where we were waiting for a friend to join us before setting off for St. Martin-in-the-Fields to lead a Healing Service there. The friend was very late in arriving and my mind could not get away from the problems we were then having to face at home. Suddenly I had a strange feeling that, although I had not told him, Godfrey knew! As that feeling came to me Godfrey broke the silence. "George, would it help if I sent you a small cheque?"

Though mine was not a health problem I know that many who had one received help from him in a way not dissimilar from this. He seemed to have a perfect attunement with heaven and out of that attunement he developed a quite extraordinary ability to read the hearts of those who sought his help.

Sometimes he would sit with people in hospital. They all felt the healing touch of his presence and many made remarkable recoveries. Some were healed who medically ought not to have been. Amongst them were patients of the late Lord Horder, physician to the King, who spoke of it to William Temple, the then Archbishop of Canterbury. Through the years the work that Godfrey did—or, rather, the quality of the life that he lived—has woven itself into the whole fabric of the Churches' Council as it is today.

If such people can convey a healing power, how much more can this be so on the level of the divine! Wherever He went, Jesus left behind a trail of lives made whole and better for His passing. As St. Matthew reminds us, "He went about healing all manner of sickness and disease among the people." In perfect attunement with the Father He was filled with the flow of all the healing energies of God at work in the universe.

The very name of Jesus spells healing. It means "God saves" or "God heals". No other name could have been more descriptive of the nature of our Lord or of the power that flowed through Him wherever He went. There was nothing strange or extraordinary about this. From the standpoint of what He was and of the gospel He came to bring could we possibly expect anything else?

The name of Jesus takes up and fulfils the whole theme of the Old Testament where one of the names by which God reveals Himself and His relationship towards us is Jehovah—Rapha, "I am the Lord that healeth thee" (Exodus 15, 26). So, in the healing work of Jesus we see God taking the initiative. Long before we ever began to search for healing the answer was there. Through His perfect attunement with the Father Jesus was allowing God to do what He always wanted and wants to do. So, we do not have to plead with Him as though He were reluctant to heal, nor do we have to strain our prayers as though He had to be persuaded to change His attitude towards us. Jesus made this perfectly clear. Being in perfect attunement with God He was filled with a continuous stream of healing energy that touched with power and transformed the lives of all who came to Him in faith.

We shall be considering the part that faith plays in later chapters. All that need be said at the moment is that it is not faith that heals. What faith does is to realise and appropriate what is already there. It cannot of itself create that for which it seeks.

And what is already there is the eternal Source of all true healing, the God whom Jesus revealed so perfectly. "I come," He said, "to do the works of Him that sent me." And again, "the Father that dwelleth within me, He doeth the works." Never did He suggest, as sometimes we do, that sickness can be the will of God. Never did He refuse to give healing lest He might be found to be working against God. Never did He say to those who sought His healing touch that they must learn to accept their troubles nobly and patiently for His sake.

On the contrary, whenever He was confronted by sickness He was affronted. Sickness, like sin, was an enemy invader despoiling His Father's creation. It was something to be cast out. It always was and it always is in the very nature of Jesus to save and to heal. He has not changed. Perhaps we have!

When Jesus sends us out to heal as well as to preach He is not asking us to do anything that He did not do Himself. His healing work was as integral a part of His total ministry as His preaching. We cannot separate

Him from either. And if His church is to be truly His body, the instrument of His indwelling, it must express the fullness of His whole being and not just one part of it.

Often He cannot do the things He wants to do in us and through us because we are not prepared just to let Him be Himself. We are prepared to let Him be a preaching Christ and even a comforting Christ but we are afraid to open all the doors and really set Him free. As long as we can contain Him within the framework of our Creed, and our worship of Him within the pattern of our long proven liturgy, we feel safe. Is this the kind of body Christ's ought to be in the face of the world's need of Him today?

No congregation of Christian people becomes fully itself as the Lord of the church wants it to be until it perfectly reflects what He Himself is. Ultimately, every Christian congregation, being a local manifestation of the universal body of Christ, is called to be Christ Himself to the people of that area. *And where the presence of Christ is, there is healing.*

Whenever we bring the sick into His presence we are bringing them into a place where the power of healing always is and always has been. It does not matter if it is a place where the ministry of healing is specifically practised through anointing and the laying-on-of-hands. What does matter is that our eyes are open to see Jesus in the fullness of His glory, to see Him as one who still heals. What matters is that the doors of our understanding have been opened wide to receive "all the benefits of his passion" and not just those that through our material intellects we can easily absorb. Such a place can be wherever His presence is realised in all its fullness—and that might be in the Eucharist, or in a gathering for prayer or when we kneel quietly at our own bedside. It is not *His nature or His attitude that has to change, but ours.*

II

IN THE NAME OF JESUS

"IF HEALING DOES NOT bring glory to God, then I would not want to be connected with it." With these words a Christian doctor began his summing up of a meeting that was held to discuss the nature and purpose of healing. A good deal of reference had been made to various forms of healing exercised by psychic and spiritist healers. As chairman of the meeting I think he captured, in this sentence, the feeling of all who were present.

While he was speaking there came into my mind a recollection of the words spoken by Peter following the healing of the lame beggar who sat outside the Beautiful Gate of the Temple: "There is none other name under heaven given among men, whereby we must be saved (made whole)" (Acts 4, 12).

For the work with which we are concerned distinguishes itself from that of any esoteric kind by being stamped by the character of Christ's own presence. Healing might be laudable for its own sake but the ministry to which our Lord calls His church goes far beyond this. It is a manifestation not only of God's activity, demonstrating His loving concern for all His creation; it also proclaims the victory of Christ and expresses the nature of His kingdom. It declares that only in Jesus does God completely save and make whole.

If our ministry is indeed to be in His name, then we do not have to be concerned if we feel we have no gift of our own. Even were we to possess any it must be put on one side. When called upon to help a sufferer we have to empty ourselves of any human talent we may possess so that the healing grace that flows through to them is entirely His. At the moment of ministration—and I think particularly of the laying-on-of-hands—only one thing matters and that is to lose ourselves in a complete attunement to the divine presence.

The two words that have come to mean most to me are awareness and obedience. Awareness to the unseen, to the movement of God's Spirit in the world of nature and in the lives of those around me. Out of this awareness there develops a sensitivity to those who seek one's help so that the few words one speaks to them come more from intuition than reason. Out of this awareness comes also an inward impulsion of the Spirit that one must obey; this chiefly has to do with the manner in which the ministration is to be given. Then, in complete attunement with the surrounding presence of the living Christ, one simply obeys.

It is only afterwards, as we look back over many such ministrations, that we realise that gifts did indeed come, though we were not conscious of their presence at the time. It was not necessarily just one gift—that of healing—but of others, too. There came a gift of discernment, a gift of faith and perhaps a gift of knowledge. The Holy Spirit pours out into the midst of any given situation the gifts that are needed for that particular occasion. We don't have to bring them ourselves.

Nor do we have to be concerned about the results. To

try to exert healing, even from the best of human motives, in order to make the result successful, is only to block the flow of divine grace and to encourage the psychic element instead. Such healing might possibly give a temporary lift to the sufferer but it would not be lasting and could be harmful in the long run.

I remember a Christian nurse working in a rehabilitation centre who longed and often prayed for the gift of healing. She had a great concern for the recovery of the healing ministry. She saw a young girl whose forearm and wrist had become permanently bent and twisted following a series of convulsions. She prayed that that girl's arm might be healed. She had become a real burden of concern to her.

Some time later the nurse came to me in distress and, with great difficulty, told me what had happened. Apparently she had "ministered" to the girl by virtually forcing her to straighten her arm and telling her, at the same time, that a miracle was happening. She had physically expressed what psychically she had been trying to do. The girl had become frightened and the convulsions started again and the mother took her away.

Many years ago a bishop asked if I would see the parents of a little boy whom they had taken a few days previously to a meeting held by an itinerant "healer". I had already heard about the boy as a report of the meeting had been big news in the local paper. His parents had taken him in his wheel-chair, and the "healer", moving up and down the aisles, had taken the boy's hands and lifted him up. In the heightened emotional atmosphere he began to walk, much to the joy and amazement of all who were there. What the newspaper did not report was that this ability had stayed with him for only two or three days. What distressed the parents most was not so much the physical aspect of it all but what it had done to their child's spirit. Previously he had been very happy, now there was nothing they could do to comfort him. I do not remember the outcome, it was too long ago, but I do remember the damage this experience had done to the parents' faith and the important lesson that it taught me.

A clergyman once told me how, in his younger days, he had met James Moore Hickson, perhaps the most outstanding apostle of divine healing in this century. Mr. Hickson travelled all over the world and was much used by God in the beginnings of the church's recovery of her healing ministry. He asked Mr. Hickson what was the difference between psychic healing and divine healing. In reply he took my friend's two hands in his own and bowing his head in deep concentration he said, "This is psychic healing." After a few moments he let go his hands and then took them again. "And this is divine healing," he said. My friend, a man with sensitivity, told me there was a marked difference though it was not easy to define in words. "I only know," he told me, "that in the first instance I felt disturbed. It was as though he was exerting an overpowering effect on me. But in the second instance I felt released. There was a warmth of love flowing into my whole being and I wanted to rejoice."

It is well worth recording that Mr. Hickson often said that the healing with which we are concerned was rooted in the old hymn, "Tell me the old, old story of Jesus and His love." There was a deep humility about Mr. Hickson and whenever he ministered to sick folk it was always in the name of Jesus and in simple obedience to His command.

And what power the name of Jesus conveys! It has an authority that cannot be found elsewhere. In its uttered presence both sin and sickness begin to lose their hold. To voice His name is to introduce a whole new dimension. When deeply troubled or when lying sick in bed one has only to put His name upon one's lips and there comes a peace that no amount of persistent prayer will ever surpass. Often in personal interviews have I invoked the holy name of Jesus and just as often have I seen its effect. Sometimes it has been so dramatic that the very air around us seemed to have become charged.

There was the twelve-year-old boy who was brought to me by his vicar. We ministered to him together. His vicar told me how the little boy's grandmother had brought home with her a ouija board for the family, with whom she lived, to play with. At first they were amused to see the upturned glasses move under their hands but then they became frightened. At this point the little boy began to have fits and to behave in a manner that was entirely strange to his normal character. Fortunately, and feeling very guilty about the whole matter, they told their vicar about it.

In the holy name of Jesus we ministered to that little boy, commanding the unclean spirit to come out of him. The whole atmosphere changed as though someone had thrown a switch. The little boy shuddered and then raised his head. On his upturned face came the sweetest smile one has ever seen. We watched him walking happily away, completely released, with one hand in each of his parents' as they set out to return to their home.

As well as ministering privately to individual sufferers in the name of the Lord, I have had the privilege of taking part in many services of healing throughout the world. Invariably, in whatever country the services took place and whatever the language spoken, the divine promise was claimed: "Where two or three are gathered together in my name, there am I in the midst." And, as people came forward to kneel at the communion rails to receive a healing blessing, the ministrants laid their hands on their heads not because they had any gift of their own but only by the power and authority of our Lord's holy name. "We come to you in the name of our Lord Jesus Christ and we lay our hands upon you in simple obedience to His command, that all sickness and disease may be driven from you, in body, mind and spirit . . ."

At one such service in St. Stephen's Church, Philadelphia, where for many years a healing ministry has been exercised with abundant blessings to countless folk, there was a woman kneeling at the rails whose body began to shake and quiver as I laid my hands upon her head and spoke words similar to those just quoted. Then I went on to the next person and the next, but at that point I knew I had to return to her. She had not yet risen to her feet to return to her place in the congregation. "By the power and authority of the holy name of Jesus," I found myself saying over her, "I command this destroying spirit to give way and to come out of you." I then put my hands on her head and asked that the Holy Spirit would fill her in every part of her being, in body, mind and spirit. Suddenly she stopped quivering, took a very deep breath and, raising her arms aloft, cried out, "Jesus, Jesus! Hallelujah!" Her deep brown eyes opened wide with a wonderful joy shining from them. Her cry reverberated throughout the vast building. I heard later that she had long been afflicted by many forms of sickness and that there had been much anger and bitterness in her soul.

I thought, after that service was over, as I have often thought on similar occasions when this had happened in private interviews, of how the first disciples returned to their Lord after they had gone out in obedience to His commission into the neighbouring villages and were amazed and awed at what had happened. "Lord," they said to Jesus, "even the devils are subject unto us through thy name."

A psychiatrist who had come to such a service in Washington, Virginia, talked with me afterwards. He was the doctor in charge of the city's drug clinic and had thousands of young addicts under his care. He was convinced that the only real answer to the problem was to be found in services like this. "We can help in the healing process," he told me, "by giving medicines, but only the power of the living Christ can really heal them. That power was here in this service." He was trying to urge universities to make a thorough medical research project into the healing ministry and especially in its relation to the drug problem.

He was impressed by what was happening in the Jesus Movement. These young people, so often unattached to any church, had discovered a power in the name of Jesus that could overcome drug addiction and many thousands had found complete release and a new purpose in life through His name.

While it is sad that so many of these young people have not yet found their true destiny in the life of the church I believe that in course of time they will. Meantime we have to remember the reply of Jesus to His disciples when they were confronted by a similar problem: "Forbid him not: for he that is not against us is for us" (Luke 9, 50).

To use the name of Jesus is to open the channel through which the God who made us and all creation can pour His saving and His healing love. In this name there is safety, power and peace. No other grace is like His.

If I were suffering and in need of help it would not be to the psychic healer I would go, nor necessarily to the one with a natural gift of healing, but rather to the man or woman whose ministry was in the name of Jesus. Such a one would probably have experienced what it is to be broken by Christ. Such power as perhaps they once thought they might have had has long been discarded. The only thing that matters to them now is God's wondrous love and His limitless grace. The healing they would give me would be His alone. Their surrendered hands upon my head would be the wounded but powerful hands of our blessed Lord. They would be ministering to me the healing power of His perfect Kingdom entirely in His name.

III

A HEALING ATMOSPHERE

ALL ABOUT US are the creative, healing energies of God filling the universe. Ceaselessly and lovingly He upholds and sustains each one of us and all that He has made. It is only as our hearts and minds, indeed our whole beings, become alive to this wonderful and unchanging reality that we can be used as channels of His healing grace. Without this consciousness any gift for which we pray or seek would be without meaning and empty of all power.

For the kind of healing we are concerned about is not confined simply to the driving away of sickness and the alleviation of pain. Though it includes these it is much more meaningful than that. It is the manifestation of that perfect life in the unseen which is released into our fallen world by Christ's victory over all evil. It is the realised answer to our prayer, "thy kingdom come, thy will be done, on earth as it is in heaven." Healing, in its truest sense, is a fruit of the gospel.

In a television interview I was suddenly asked if I wished I had the power in my hands to rid sickness and disease from the life of every sufferer who came for help. It was an unexpected question thrown at me towards the end of the interview and quite out of context of the preceding discussion. I remember clearly the sense of dismay the question brought to me. All I could think to reply was that I would *hate it* and that far more important was the coming of Christ's kingdom into our fallen world. There the programme ended. There was no time to say any more.

I suppose we all have our ideas about what is meant by "the Kingdom". To me it is the real, though unseen, world of God's perfection. It is the world where the powers of evil have been overcome and where the sovereignty of Christ's presence pervades all. It is to this unseen world that we really and ultimately belong and in it, through Christ's victory, we can even now live, and move, and have our being. We can experience its delights when we turn aside to pray or when we enter meditatively and relaxedly into the Silence of God's eternity. It is here, in this unseen world, where healing begins.

It is always interpenetrating our world and sometimes we get clear glimpses of it. We see it in nature, we see it in human life. There are moments, for example, when a beauty not of this world breaks through and transforms the earthly scene.

I was travelling recently northwards for mile after mile of a motorway on a very dull day when the clouds were heavy and most headlights were switched on. The expectant storm suddenly broke. Through the rain-lashed windscreen the traffic looked like a fleet of fast boats power-driving their way along the surface of a lake, hurling their spray behind them. For a few miles we ploughed along together as though in a mutually agreed formation. Then, quite suddenly, the storm was over and the sun shone brilliantly from a clear sky. At that moment we had arrived at one of those stretches of the motorway where the broad banks, sloping upwards and away from the road, had been tastefully and thoughtfully landscaped. All nature seemed to be glistening with a rare and beautiful light. I don't know how the other travellers felt, but, for me, it was a moment of revelation beyond and deeper than the apparent beauty all could see. The scene was moving enough in itself but it seemed also to be bursting with a glory not of this world only. It was as though I could see beyond the apparent beauty and behold that of the unseen and perfect world of heaven breaking through. My whole being responded to it in an ecstasy of joy and I found myself sending out streams of love, God's love, to all the other travellers who were speeding along the road that day.

We experience the same kind of joy when we see a man or woman or child becoming healed by the touch of the risen Christ or when the atmosphere of a home or community becomes transformed by Him. What we see at these times is not simply a cure or release from the afflicting illness of body or mind, though often it will include that, but rather a healing of the whole situation. It is as though God's perfection, already existing in the heavenlies, breaks through the dark clouds of our imperfect life and manifests itself on earth.

I remember our early days at the Home of Healing in Crowhurst when we were faced with many problems. Among them, and more fundamental than all the others, was that of filling the Home with the atmosphere of Christ's healing love. It was not just a sentimental kind of thing I was seeking but rather the vital, cleansing and creative love which is born only of the Holy Spirit. Within such an atmosphere, could it only come, I knew that people would be healed. Within such an atmosphere, any ministrations of the laying-on-of-hands I might be called to give, and any medical assistance, would be far more effective than similar help given to them in their own homes.

What I had not reckoned with was the struggle in the spiritual realm. Unknown to me at first, though I discovered it later, the Home was being assaulted by dark forces. I know that those who have had experience in the unseen realm will understand. It is the story behind the story that I related in *Miracle at Crowhurst.**

At first, a number of things went wrong and I sensed waves of disquiet going through the Home. Members of the staff became distraught for no apparent reason; one, in a very responsible position, suffered acute abdominal pains which baffled the doctor. I would go into the large kitchen and stand quietly by the window out of people's way, for there was much coming and going. I don't remember how long I would stand there but I was always conscious of an inner struggle before the forces of God's peace prevailed. I would enter into the unseen world of Christ's kingdom, calling upon the Holy Spirit to drive out all evil and flood the whole building with His light and love. After a while I knew the struggle was over and sometimes I was given to "see" holy angels overshadowing and protecting the Home.

Towards the end of this period I had a brief encounter with the woman who had been the chief human agent in this assault on the Home. Her eyes blazing with hatred, she cried, "Your magic is stronger than mine!" She died from a series of heart attacks soon afterwards, though not before I had had an opportunity to confront her compassionately with the forgiving love of the gospel of our Lord.

The most memorable event of this phase came at the

*Published by Arthur James Ltd., Evesham, Worcs.

end of it. I was not the only one conscious of what was happening. Though I had not spoken of it, one or two members of the staff told me of their own suspicions. Before the woman died we decided to close the Home for a couple of weeks, ostensibly for re-decoration and repairs, but in fact to give us a chance of dealing with the situation and making a fresh start. The most important thing was a service of cleansing and blessing. The staff met in the little chapel, as it then was, and from there we went into every room in the house. Finally, we returned to the chapel to give thanks; as we did so, the birds in the trees outside burst into song although it was a dreary and bitterly cold January day!

From that moment we were all aware of a new atmosphere filling the house. Many visitors remarked on it. Even the tradesmen spoke of it. I was glad they felt that love was there and the spirit of healing, too. They never knew what lay behind it. God's heavenly perfection in the unseen world about us was breaking through.

I have come to know most of our Homes and centres of healing here and abroad. It is strange, yet perhaps not so strange, that all of them go through periods of severe trial. It seems that anyone concerned with the real work of the Kingdom in all its fullness attracts assaults from evil powers.

But it is not only in Homes and centres of Healing, where most people would expect to find an atmosphere of healing, that such things happen. There are also congregations and Christian families and individuals who have come through a time of trial and who know, as a result of that experience, the unshakeable peace of heaven.

I think, for example, of St. Stephen's in Philadelphia. This church was almost being made redundant when the Rev. Dr. Alfred Price asked if it might be kept open a little longer, while he took over as its rector. In the old days it had been a lively church but its congregation had moved into the suburbs. What remained of its residential area was now filled with the riff-raff of the city. Brothels abounded. The police were powerless.

Alfred finally came to the conclusion that there was only one thing that mattered. That Christ be upheld in all His glory as Healer and Lord. He painstakingly visited all the houses in the red-light area. They laughed at him; they poured scorn on him. They did all they could to get him out. But Alfred believed that miracles can happen. He knew his Lord. And because he believed they could happen, they did!

First one and then another of the "girls" came to him for help until, in time, many of them did. The word spread that here was someone who could love with the love of Jesus. One by one the red lights went out until the whole area was cleared. What the police had been unable to do, the power of the risen Christ had done. Alfred started to hold services of healing, uplifting the Lord in all His fullness, and folk came into the church, as Alfred puts it, right off the sidewalks to see what was happening. They saw, they were deeply affected and they stayed. The work has long been well-established and is now led by Alfred's successor, the Rev. Roy Hendricks. From all over America and beyond folk go there, nowadays, to seek the healing touch of the risen Lord.

As well as places there are occasions, too, when it seems that the power of the kingdom is very near, times when the atmosphere becomes charged. Some of these occasions were, perhaps, expected or half expected. We were caught up in a movement of the Spirit and the world of the unseen pressed in upon us.

Such occasions invariably happen when a group of churches join together for a mission of healing, especially during the final gathering. After two or three days of teaching, a service of healing is held and the clergy and ministers give the laying-on-of-hands to all present. For we all need healing! The services often seem to be reminiscent of the event recorded by St. Luke when "the power of the Lord was present to heal". There was something in the atmosphere that could not be defined in any other way. Everyone felt it. And the significant thing about that occasion was not specifically healing. He was teaching. He was opening the eyes of His hearers' understanding to the unseen world of God's perfection.

There is no doubt that the Lord is blessing these missions and services of healing. Clergy often tell me, especially if they have never participated before, that they were more conscious of our Lord's presence while ministering the laying-on-of-hands than at any other time or any other service. There is no doubt, too, about the atmosphere of love and power that is released in them. It touches everyone present. Following such a service recently in the south of England a young woman wrote to me, "The service was a vast gathering at the feet of Jesus. The experience of His presence was the answer to all our questions. Testimonies to blessing and healing are still coming in, but the joy of it all is that we know in our hearts that the healing power of Jesus was released and that great things happened."

You don't have to be terribly sensitive to atmospheres to know that something *extra*-ordinary is happening. I have seen tears of release and joy fall from the eyes of many a hard-headed business man as he rose from his knees after having received the healing touch of Christ through the laying-on-of-hands.

In such an atmosphere a healing has often begun long before the time the congregation is invited to the communion rails for the laying-on-of-hands. There was the blind woman who was brought by her friend. During the address near the beginning of the service something happened to her. Suddenly, for the first time for many years, she began to see light and the people around her were like dark shadows moving. After she had knelt to receive the laying-on-of-hands she could see more clearly still.

There was the aged nun suffering badly from arthritis who had come to the service thinking she might be among those who would receive while still sitting in the pews. Usually, after ministering the laying-on-of-hands to those who come to the communion rails, the ministrants go down into the congregation. However, during the address and again during the prayers, she felt a loosening in her limbs. She began to wonder if, after all, she might manage to climb the steps leading to the rails and, though still unable to kneel, receive the laying-on-of-hands while standing there. So when the invitation was given she joined the queue waiting to go up and gradually went towards the rails. With great excitement she managed to climb the steps unaided and then her turn came to go forward. When she reached the rails she found herself able to bend her knees and, joy of joys, to kneel before her Lord as easily as anyone else, as she had not done for a very long time.

In such cases, which happen so often, the ensuing ministration, which ends the service, seems to set the seal of Christ's name on the healing that has already begun. The ministration is like the divine imprimatur, the heavenly amen.

The greatest value of these services lies not so much in the healings that take place but in the atmosphere that is created through the upholding of the risen Christ in all His glory. All who come, the healthy and the sick, are affected. Many who might now be sick are not so—during such a service they have been released from predisposing factors of stress that would ultimately result in disease.

"I, if I be lifted up," promised Jesus, "will draw all men unto me." And that is precisely what happens. He is the divine magnet who draws to Himself those who are sick in mind, body or soul, those who have lost their way in life and those who are suffering from the stresses and strains of today. People travel long distances to attend the services. They come because they are sincerely, and in some instances desperately, seeking healing that only the Lord can give.

The services provide opportunities for the teaching and the preaching of the gospel, especially that concerning the healing ministry; they are far more effective than at any other time. A private interview is not the best time for teaching. It is a time for listening and sharing. Here, the emphasis is on the sufferer and his troubles; and such verbal teaching as is given is minimal. But in a public service the emphasis is on the Christ, risen and ascended, and His victory over all evil. It is designed to lift the minds and hearts of the congregation on to a higher plane. Here they learn what the meaning of healing truly is, and what part they themselves can play in the healing ministry and in intercessory prayer. The meaning of the church being the body of Christ really comes alive.

No one can assess the unspoken teaching that the Holy Spirit gives through the atmosphere generated in these services and the act of the laying-on-of-hands in the Lord's name. It is abundantly clear that the teaching He gives to the hearts and minds and souls of those who come goes deeper and far more effectively than anything said from the pulpit.

I pray and long for the time when every service in every church will have this atmosphere. Perhaps this is an impossible dream, but who knows, as this fuller gospel continues to grow and spread through all the churches, what effect it may eventually have? I know many churches whose ordinary services have quite a different atmosphere now from what they used to have. Services of healing are regularly held and a spirit of expectancy has entered into them.

On the desk or hanging on the office walls of some American business men I have seen the slogan, "Expect a Miracle!" Where this expectancy exists miracles can and do happen. For the Lord can do with us and in us only so much as we are prepared to allow Him to do. If the eyes of the congregation have been opened to the reality of Christ's healing power, then every service and every meeting together in His name becomes a service of healing. Expectancy releases His power. And where expectancy is, there the power of the Lord is present to heal.

A great responsibility falls, of course, upon the minister. If he is a man who really believes that with Christ all things are possible then his belief will be conveyed to his congregation, whatever words he may use. The spirit behind the words will have its own impact. A doctor friend once told me that the attitude of his patients towards him changed wonderfully after the day when he came to accept Jesus as the great Healer of men. They became much more open with him. Somehow his belief was mysteriously conveyed to them. But sometimes it is not so much the minister as the officers of the church who hold greatest sway. They can encourage or, more tragically, block the flow of Christ's healing power and the moving of His Spirit in a congregation. But, if both they and the minister genuinely believe that Christ is the same, yesterday, today and forever, and together expect great things, then miracles *can* and do happen!

IV

THE SPRINGS OF HEALING

ONE OF THE MARKS of a great work of literature is that you can read it again and again. Every time you do so it reveals things you could vow were not there before. Though the gospels are not just works of literature they certainly share this quality.

You can read the accounts of our Lord's healing work a thousand times and see in them nothing more than miracles attesting the fact that He is the Messiah. But if at some point in your life the healing events in the gospel become an up-to-date reality you see in them something more exciting still. You become conscious of an ordered and orderly law operating in the unseen realm of which Jesus is the supreme Master.

In a sense we thus become like St. Luke when he wrote his account of our Lord's life. Though he was not an eye-witness yet, nevertheless, we are left with the impression that here is a man with a doctor's eye for detail and a doctor's heart of compassion and understanding, watching closely the work of the Supreme Master of healing. Further, he sees in the work of Jesus a dimension of healing that cannot be defined within the limits of *materia medica* alone.

He records how, on one occasion, "there was a woman which had a spirit of infirmity eighteen years, and was bowed together [literally, bent double], and could in no wise lift herself up" (Luke 13, 11). Without His being asked to help, Jesus took the initiative and called her to Him. After He had healed her and been accused by the ruler of the synagogue for having done this on the Sabbath day, Jesus said: "Ought not this woman . . . whom Satan hath bound . . . be loosed from this bond?"

Perhaps we do not think, nowadays, of anyone having a *spirit* of infirmity. We would probably say she was suffering from acute arthritis, a physical thing. We might blame the damp conditions of her cottage home or perhaps her own inner responses to what life had brought to her. Today we might think of it as a stress disorder; yesterday we might have thought it psychosomatic. Had she lived today she might have been able to benefit from specific treatments available to arthritic sufferers. Certainly we would not think of her as being "possessed".

Yet I sometimes wonder who is nearer the truth —Luke, who himself was a doctor, or the strictly medical opinion of our own materialistic age? I suspect the answer lies in how deeply we look into the cause of illness. What is its nature and how do we assess it? On the surface this woman was suffering from a well-known physical disease, but what lay behind her particular trouble? What, on a deeper level lies behind all sickness and disease?

It seems to me that when we view sickness from the point of view of the Kingdom we see three levels. First, the obvious one of the sickness itself; this we can describe by some particular label—asthma, arthritis, cancer or something else. Secondly, there is that of the underlying causes with their eventual precipitating factors; these are often of a spiritual or emotional nature. Thirdly, there is the level which we observe only by our Christian intuition as we recognise that we wrestle not simply with the sufferer's own problems but "against powers, against the rulers of the darkness of this world".

It is the first and the second level that take most of our time and energies. So often behind the illness there seem to lie wrong attitudes to the hurts of life. We bury them deep inside ourselves, unable to fight or to run away from them, and we just do not know how to assimilate them in a positive and creative manner. Eventually they reach a bursting point. They just have to be externalised one way or another. If we are fortunate we find someone with understanding who can share the burden, but, if not, the hurt expresses itself, as if by way of relief, in our physical body.

Take asthma as an example. Many who suffer from this distressing disease are young people who generally grow out of it, but occasionally it persists into adult age. Is it fear that lies behind it? We cannot say with certainty, but time and again we get the feeling that the child within, however old he may be, is perpetually afraid that he will never be able to catch up with the demands he thinks society is imposing upon him. In young people society is usually represented by his parents or teachers.

Take arthritis. Again, we cannot speak with absolute certainty. Every sufferer is unique. But we find ourselves asking if the underlying cause might not be a long period of buried resentment—a mixture of anger and frustration. I have ministered to countless people suffering from this illness and during the course of the interviews I have noticed how often there is a deep feeling that life has not treated them fairly.

Finally, cancer. Is the precipitating cause a deep hurt in what one might call the love-area of a sufferer's being? When we were born we were all brought into being, but not all were brought into a state of well-being. Some never knew the deep security of being really wanted, and, *through the years, there has been a vulnerability in this basic sphere of life.* Though I never take case notes of all the sufferers, a general impression remains. So many have been those to whom the giving and receiving of love have meant more than to most. Obviously, other factors might also be involved that are purely physical and may even be connected with heredity, and these may have precipitated the trouble; but it is so often the "nice people" who are hit by this disease.

Turning from one disease to another, I generally find that what initially brought the sufferer to look for help was simply the consequence of a deeper state of dis-ease, of an unhappy inner-conflict long buried. Though the helper is aware of this, it is not his primary business to carry out an analysis of the situation. He may be led to ask questions here and there as the story unfolds. This is not just to establish the cause of the trouble. It is to evoke memories of hurts that happened perhaps long ago.

On these two levels the description "Christian counselling" is perhaps sufficient. But when it comes to ministering the healing touch of Christ through prayer, the laying-on-of-hands or holy unction, we are taking part in something far more profound than counselling. Bringing ourselves into an utter attunement with the unseen world of Christ's kingdom we are channelling into the sufferer's being the fruits of Christ's victory in the deepest level, too.

It is into an appreciation of this third level of sickness that the work of healing done in obedience to our Lord's command ultimately brings us. I do not think it is possible for any Christian whose heart and mind are moved by the love of Christ to enter empathetically into a deep relationship with one sufferer after another over a long period without eventually becoming aware of the diabolical origins of all sickness and disease. It is right that a doctor should be aware of the first two levels, the illness itself and the underlying causes that precipitate it; but if we engage ourselves in our Lord's ministry of healing we cannot stop there. Inevitably, the Spirit of Christ moving within us will bring to our consciousness the stark realisation that here, on this third level, we are confronted by a manifestation of evil itself.

It is just here that we see the real relationship between sickness and sin. Together, they emanate from the fall. They are the twin destroyers of God's creation. Often it is not the sufferer himself who has sinned. His sickness is not a punishment. It is not necessarily the result of some evil he has done or some good he has failed to do. Too many other factors are involved for the blame to be laid at his door. Time and again, I have thought when sitting with a sufferer and listening to his story that he is more sinned against than sinning. Had I been given his upbringing, and his circumstances, experiencing similar hurts, I might now be sitting where he sits. In effect, towards the end of an interview, both helper and sufferer are united in a bond of identification, looking together at the mess evil has made of God's wonderful creation.

Realising this, we are following in our Lord's footsteps by being allowed to share a little in His view of life and in His attitude towards suffering. He recognised all disease as being, in origin, an evil thing. For He could see, as His Father could see, a world made perfect. He looked at everything that He had made, and behold, it was very good! In every single one of us, and, indeed, in all creation, He could see the perfection and the glory that is His Father's perfect will. That glory had been horribly despoiled.

No wonder, then, that time and again, as we watch Him when confronted by sickness and disease, we become conscious of a mighty rising of anger interwoven with His compassion. There is a divine necessity about His healing work that cannot be denied.

I feel strongly that when Jesus said, "I will, be thou clean", in response to the leper's "If it be thy will, thou canst heal me", His words were not softly spoken but, rather, that they burst forth from Him. He looked with a great compassion on the poor man standing there, but seeing beneath and beyond the sickness itself to its original and destructive source, He loudly proclaimed, "I will! be thou clean!"

There is an interesting and telling word used here in this incident when we look at the Greek from which our New Testaments have been translated. It is pronounced "*stenatzo*". It appears again on two other occasions. It comes in the incident when Jesus healed the man who was deaf and dumb (Mark 7, 32-37) and again when He raised Lazarus from the dead (John 11). The word "*stenatzo*" speaks of "a gathered power". Translators have always had difficulty in putting it into English. In the story of the healing of the leper it has been variously translated as "moved with compassion" and as "moved with anger". In that of the man who was deaf and dumb it is translated as Jesus "sighed", and in the raising of Lazarus from the dead, where it is a little stronger, as Jesus "groaned in the spirit".

Literally, the word means "to snort with anger", and my Greek scholar friends tell me that although it is not the kind of word one would expect to find in the New Testament, least of all in connection with Jesus, it is to be found in the pages of classical Greek. Here it is used for the snorting of a horse.

Imagine a horse tethered in a stable and the stable catches fire. There develops in the horse a gathering of power, its strong muscles quiver and there is a great stamping of its hooves. Suddenly, with a loud snort, the animal bursts its bonds, breaks through the stable doors and is free.

It seems to me that on the occasions when Jesus heals the leper and restores hearing and speech to the man who was deaf and dumb, He has entered right into the midst of the sufferer's situation, and in perfect identification with him, bursts through the bondage of his sickness. In the third instance, that of the raising of Lazarus, He is entering even the portals of death itself. On each of these occasions there is a great gathering of power and Jesus "snorts". "Be healed!" He commands the leper; "*Ephphatha!*" He calls out to the deaf and dumb man; and, with a loud voice, "Come forth!" He cries out to the entombed Lazarus. In each case the bonds are broken and the man is set free.

For when Jesus heals it is not with some strange and gentle power imposed from without. He enters right into our situation, sharing it with us and taking into Himself the sin and sickness by which we are bound, and breaks evil's hold. As Cardinal Newman's lovely hymn of praise puts it:

O generous love! That He, who smote
In man for man the foe,
The double agony in man
For man should undergo.

There were many people then, as now, who could not understand His healing work. They were embarrassed and puzzled by it. Not for them was there the intellectual escape into the realms of mythology! They were brought face to face with it and it made the religious leaders particularly uncomfortable. The pharisees, at least realising that the springs of His power came from a very deep level, accused that His healing work was done by the power of Beelzebub.

But the firm reply of Jesus silenced them. "If I, by the finger of God, cast out devils," He told them, "no doubt the kingdom of God is come upon you!" He then goes on to tell them that, with His coming, a power greater than that of Satan had entered into the world, and it was by this power he loosed men from their bonds. "When a strong man armed keepeth his palace, his goods are in peace: but when a stronger than he shall come upon him, and overcome him, he taketh from him all his armour wherein he trusted, and divideth his spoils" (Luke 11, 21-22).

The healing ministry of Jesus is, therefore, something more than just a proof of His Messiahship and even more than just that of a great healer bringing release and happiness to a few sick folk in Galilee long ago. He was demonstrating that in Him the power of a new dimension had entered into this fallen world. Every healing work that He performed was a proclamation of His gospel. It was a "sign", as St. John puts it, of the glorious activity of His Kingdom.

In this Kingdom there is victory over the forces of evil. The followers of our Lord are sent out into the world to take its fruits to all men everywhere and till the end of time. In Him a new age has dawned and we are commissioned to proclaim it as much by healing the sick in His name as by our preaching and teaching. We are called not to resignation in the face of suffering but to an active hostility towards it.

A clergyman who recently took part for the first time in a public service of healing where a large crowd of people was present wrote to me afterwards about the effect it had had upon him. Obviously, he had been expecting, as do so many who have never been to one, something quite different.

"It was not," he wrote, "simply a re-enactment of the Capernaum scene which is so vividly but rather sentimentally portrayed in the hymn, 'At even ere the sun was set', but rather a demonstration of Christ's victory and power over the forces of evil. It didn't seem to matter whether those who attended and came up to receive the laying-on-of-hands were in wheel-chairs or apparently well. We were all in the fight together. For the first time in my ministry I was able to see sickness clearly for what it truly is—a work not of God but of those forces of evil which are opposed to His loving will for us all. I felt myself that I was being called to a new ordination."

It was this aspect of our Lord's healing work that struck St. Luke when commenting on the woman with "a spirit of infirmity". As a doctor St. Luke may have had his own estimate of her troubled condition and even known of some treatment that might have been given her. This would have had its own importance. For the doctor, in his dedication to overcome sickness and disease, is on God's side and, therefore, plays a vital part in the total ministry of healing. But whatever might have been his attitude from the medical point of view it is clear that as a man he recognises in Jesus someone who can look beneath the surface of things and whose authority knows no bounds.

If, as followers of Jesus, we exercise the healing ministry in His name and by the authority He has committed to His church, we shall inevitably become conscious of all three levels of suffering whenever we are confronted by sickness. Though we may be more immediately aware of the first two levels—the sufferer's apparent need and the inner state of dis-ease that lies behind it—there will always be the realisation that here we are faced by evil and destructive powers at work in the third and deepest level.

I am sure that where such an awareness exists there comes a greater power in the ministration we give. Somehow there is mysteriously conveyed into the core of the sufferer's being a realisation that a power not of this world is entering in. It is as though the evil beneath the suffering recognises its Conqueror. The Holy Spirit conveys messages into the heart of the sufferer that are more powerful and profound than any we ourselves, however dedicated, could ever possibly give.

But, as the ministrant enters empathetically into the total situation of the sufferer he is trying to help, he will also experience within himself something of that deep groaning of the spirit which our Lord Himself knew. It is perhaps a sharing in the Lord's own self-emptying when, in identifying Himself with us in our sufferings, He became man. Using the Greek word I call this a "*kenotic*" experience (Philippians 2, 5-8). Such an experience will often come in the hour preceding our meeting with a friend who is desperately ill. Similarly, if the ministrants who are to take part in a public service of healing previously experience a feeling of desolation and of being emptied of all power of their own, they can be comforted by realising that only so can the fullness of Christ's glory and victory flow through them. As we follow in His healing steps we are called to share with Him, as members of His body, in His sufferings that we may share, also, in the joys of His resurrection power.

In the entrance hall of "de hezenburg", the Home of Healing in Hattem, Holland, hangs a large painting. It is a picture of a deep pit, surrounded by cliffs, into which a man has fallen. Around and on top of the cliffs sit various well-known figures offering help and advice. One, for example, is Confucius, who, in great sadness for the fallen man, is telling him that if only he had followed his teaching he would not be where he is now. Another is the Buddha expounding the values of meditation wherein he would find peace in his hapless condition. But there is another figure and this one is no longer on the cliff-side. He has climbed down into the pit itself, his cloak bespattered with the mud, and he is coming to the exact spot where the fallen man lies. Needless to say, this other figure, entering into the fallen man's own situation and sharing it with him, is Jesus.

V

THE WORKS OF GOD

JESUS AND HIS DISCIPLES once found themselves confronted by a man who had been blind from birth. His disciples asked Him, "Who did sin, this man or his parents, that he was born blind?" (John 9, 1-3). Though they had little knowledge of what we would describe as the psychosomatic cause of illness, they did have some idea about the laws of cause and effect. They wanted to know what lay behind the trouble.

It would have been very interesting to read Jesus' analysis of how this particular illness had come about and His insights into these tremendous questions. There were at least two occasions when He seemed to imply that the sickness with which He had been confronted had been linked with wrong thoughts or attitudes. To one sufferer He said, after He had healed him at the pool of Bethesda, "Sin no more, lest a worse thing befall thee" (John 5, 14). To the man sick of the palsy He said, "Thy sins are forgiven thee" (Mark 2, 5). Perhaps the first had been wrong in his attitude to life. He had enjoyed being ill. And it may be that the man sick of the palsy had been paralysed from a deep sense of guilt rising into fear.

But the reply of Jesus was not on the level of His disciples' question. He seemed to be looking at the blind man's situation from an entirely different viewpoint. Instead of staying to discuss the whys and wherefores of the man's illness He gives the reply, "that the works of God might be seen in him".

There was a dimension in His thinking, in His whole attitude to the situation, that was not in theirs. Other factors were present that they could not see. And these were far more important than the obvious. His reply lifted the situation on to a higher level altogether.

Whatever its cause might have been, God had not permitted evil to enter into this world without providing another power which could bring victory over it. It was this other power that was so clear to Jesus. He looked with eyes that were not limited to the boundary of our human understanding. He could see men not only from the viewpoint of this world but also from that of His perfect kingdom. He could see them not only as they were, hurt by this world, but also as they might be, as God wanted them to be. For Him there was only one ultimate answer to the question of men's suffering. It was, as Jesus said, that the works of God might be seen in them.

His answer was positive and practical and it is this kind of answer His followers are called to give. As we minister in His name we know that another factor is breaking through into the situation. Not that we know beforehand exactly what the effect of Christ's victory over evil is going to be. We cannot predict or predetermine what His power will do. But we listen, we share and we minister in the power of His name. That is all He calls us to do. The results are His, and sometimes they are more wonderful than we dare to think.

There was the surgeon who brought his young wife to a healing mission in Richmond, Virginia. They had travelled many miles that Sunday morning in the hope that something might be done for her. As we sat in the comfortable chairs of the rector's vestry the surgeon, holding his wife's hand as she bravely tried to hold back the tears, told me of their trouble. I learned that he had lost his first wife from cancer and now this, his second wife, was suffering from the same disease. They were an ideally happy couple, obviously much in love with life and with each other. At home they had two small children waiting for them.

The main service was due to begin in half an hour, so I listened, I shared, I felt something of the weight of their burden and then ministered in our Lord's name to them both.

It was not until I returned to England about a month later that I heard of them again. Some ten days after we had met that Sunday morning she had been suddenly rushed off to hospital by ambulance suffering severe pains in the lower abdomen. There was an immediate operation and it was discovered that the cancerous tissue had broken free from its host and was trying to find its way by natural means out of her body. In a few moments it was removed. For all who were concerned for this young couple, the rector and his prayer group and the doctors who operated, there was cause for great rejoicing.

I remember others who were not so wonderfully released. The disease remained. But there came such a great change into their situations that often the people closest to them marvelled. The physical pain they ought from the medical point of view to have suffered did not happen and a new spiritual radiance transformed them. Fear became replaced by peace, and self-concern by love. A power and a glory not of this world had entered in.

In other words, whatever the suffering might be, and however it came about, evil has not the final word. The final answer is God's and what the power of God can make of it. Admit Him into a situation and that situation itself becomes changed. The "how" of it all comes to have little more than academic interest. Indeed, we might well say that the only thing that makes sense of sin and sickness, if anything does, is God's cleansing and healing grace.

Perhaps the young Baptist minister I met recently had found the secret. He and his wife had been looking forward to the birth of their first child and his whole congregation had shared the joy of anticipation with them. The baby came, a little girl, and they were showered with presents. But a few weeks later they realised their baby would be a backward child. She suffered from a congenital disease. The shock, in which so many friends were involved, hit them badly. He told me how he and his wife had wrestled agonisingly with the question, "Why should this have happened to us?" Both of them experienced deep feelings of guilt, wondering why the God whom they trusted and served had treated them like this. Despite the sympathy of the congregation they went through a very dark time and experienced considerable distress. Then, quite suddenly, it happened. "Something clicked in my mind," he told me, "and I found myself asking, 'Why should this not have happened to us?' "

He told his wife about it, and to his joy, found that the same thought had come to her at just about the same time. "From that moment," he told me, "everything was different. *We knew that what we had been given was not a burden but a very great privilege. The Lord had called us to take a share in the world's suffering that we might take a share also in His victory.* If we were truly Christian we ought to be able to accept the challenge that so many other young parents today have to accept in a positive manner. It could happen to anyone, so why should it not happen to us?"

My young friend has found a second vocation, no less important in his eyes than his first. And I have no doubt at all that the works of God are going to become more and more evident in the life of that young man both as a father and as a pastor of souls.

VI

THE CAPTAIN OF OUR SALVATION

INVARIABLY WHEN I AM ASKED, "Why should this have happened to me?" there flashes into my mind a picture of the Christ upon His cross. If ever anybody had the right to ask, it was He. He knew no sin. He never hurt anyone. His whole life was lived in perfect obedience to His Father's will. Why should He be punished? And here we come face to face with the great imponderables with which philosophers and theologians have wrestled through the ages.

If ever there was a situation of utter desperation it happened on Calvary hill. But never have we seen more clearly "the works of God" springing out of it.

I think of all that it has inspired—of the thousands of beautiful paintings and gem-studded crucifixes and crosses that artists have fashioned through the generations since. I think of the majesty of our vast cathedrals and the glory of our hymns and oratorios. I think of the countless men and women who, through its inspiration, have risen to heights of manhood never known before.

We all get hurt. Jesus never promised His followers that they would escape. Though we may live and move and have our being in His Kingdom we are still, for these "threescore years and ten", part and parcel of this world. It is no use dreaming of flying away to some paradise island to find freedom. As long as we live in this life we shall always know what we might call the sin of this fallen world.

Sooner or later we shall come to experience what is meant by grief and stress. And time and again we shall need the touch of healing grace that only Christ can give.

The wonderful thing is that He has been through it all Himself. He shared in the grief surrounding Lazarus's death; there was a note of grief in His voice as, at the end of His ministry on earth, He called out, "O Jerusalem, you who stoned the prophets and killed them that were sent unto you, how oft would I have gathered you as a hen gathereth her chickens under her wings, but ye would not." And surely there must have been grief when one of His own betrayed Him, the others forsook Him and He was left utterly alone.

There is a startling phrase in the Epistle to the Hebrews (2, 10): "It behoved God to make the captain of our salvation perfect through suffering." There are two thoughts here. The first is that it was only through His experience of every aspect of human life, its joys and its sufferings, that Jesus could attain perfect manhood. The second is that only by so doing could He be the saviour and healer of us all.

I sometimes think of varying depths of suffering as strata in a rock. Some of us can live a lifetime without entering very deeply into suffering, while others experience it at deeper levels. Jesus descended into the lowest stratum of all.

Not even the saints and martyrs experienced the depth of suffering He knew. For them there was always the realisation of an unseen presence to strengthen them. But at that supreme moment on the cross when

Jesus cried out in anguish, "My God, my God, why hast thou forsaken me?" He looked around and beneath for a hand to support Him, but there was none. There was nothing but infinite emptiness. He was supremely alone.

That is why there is always Someone who can understand. Whatever depth of suffering comes our way the Christ still stands-under. He always knows just how and where we are. There is no place where He has not been Himself.

Studdert Kennedy, the popular padre of the 1914-18 war, better known as Woodbine Willie, was asked by a soldier who had been badly wounded what kind of a God it was that allowed such suffering. Studdert Kennedy showed him the little crucifix he kept in his pocket. The soldier gazed at it for a few moments then quietly said, "Now, I understand."

Earlier we were thinking how the very name of Jesus speaks of God's initiative in bringing about a way for us into salvation-wholeness. Here, as we think of this text from the Epistle to the Hebrews, we are reminded of that other "captain of salvation", who bore the same name, though we pronounce it Jeshua or Joshua. For years the Jews had been in bondage seeking a way of escape but, unable to find one themselves they yearned for freedom. God then took the initiative. So does He do that for us now. Unable of ourselves to find a way of escape from the bondage of our sufferings, God sends us, in Jesus, a captain of our salvation. In Him, and in Him alone, is our healing, our strength and our peace. He it is who leads us out of bondage and into a land flowing with milk and honey.

If we are called to suffer grief it is no good fighting against it or trying to run away from it. Just like any other hurt that comes to us we have somehow to learn that the only way to victory is by assimilating it into our total experience of life. When Jesus told us to take up our cross He was not just saying something pious. He was showing us the way to deal triumphantly with it.

Grief, strangely enough, is a medicine. Like laughter and tears it is part of our mechanism. We may have to put on a brave face in front of others, but there must also be times when we just have to let it have its own way. The tears must fall and the heart beneath must be allowed to feel and accept its brokenness.

I have known dear good Christian people who have continued to suffer long after their loss, either because others were afraid to go near them and treated them almost like lepers or, when they did talk with them, instead of helping, encouraged them to believe that the proper Christian attitude was to keep a "stiff upper lip"!

A relative of mine once suffered like this. She and her husband were stalwarts in their church and were well known for their charity. He was struck down at the height of a distinguished medical career. She was given no time to mourn. She was expected to set a "good Christian example" and she responded. I was a young boy at the time and wondered why we never heard very much of her afterwards. I learned later that she had had a bad mental breakdown, from which she never recovered.

My first experience of grief was when, as a boy of fourteen, I lost my mother. I was away at school and I remember the headmaster calling me into his study to tell me the news. It was a shock. I thought the world had come to an end. What I could not understand was the attitude of friends of the family who always used to talk with me but did not after that. I felt in quarantine. Loneliness became my bedfellow. Under cover of the blankets I would cry like any other boy.

But I remember becoming dimly conscious even then of something I have certainly learned since. It is that somewhere in us there is an indestructible point that links directly to the Source of all being and of all creation. I do not know what to call it. Perhaps psyche is the nearest word.

So, whenever we go through a time of grief we can enter into its suffering, not fighting against it or trying to run away from it, but savouring its essence, till we reach that point beneath where we are at one with God Himself. This is, above all others, a place of healing. For there is grief, too, in the heart of God. Here, our grief can be relinquished into His. In Jesus He has broken through into grief's domain and has conquered its power.

It takes time, but grief can be absorbed and its burden brought under control. It is like reining in a runaway horse. We do not suddenly pull him to a halt but there comes a time when we know it can be done. Then such manhood as we may have becomes deepened and enriched. What began as a seemingly intolerable loss has been turned into gain.

Stress, in its various forms, is on the increase and it is very likely that it will become worse. Every now and then new inventions are supposed to make life easier. Instead, they increase its speed so that we are made to go faster and faster. Standards, too, rise higher every year, in science, academics generally, art and sport. I am amazed when I see the examination papers our young people at universities and in colleges have to pass. No wonder some of them have breakdowns and others drop out. I can understand, too, why some of my business friends talk about the spiritual nature of the game of golf. In playing it they find escape from the pressures of their jobs, release from the mental and physical tensions and a relaxation of spirit in nature's beauty and healing balm.

The cause of stress can perhaps best be illustrated by the strings of a violin. Each one is made to its particular specification and when tightened to that degree of tension for which it was made is ready to do its perfect work. Each of us is separately designed to perform his best work when the right degree of tension is reached. If the violin string is too tense or too slack, when it is played it cannot do the work for which it is made. Then it must be unwound and allowed to relax that its texture may not be harmed.

We, too, are made to a particular specification. Each one is unique. Stress comes usually from one of two causes. Either because the pressures on us are such that we are in a continual state of tension so that we never have periods to relax or do not know how to, or because we are being over-tensed in order to produce a performance for which we were not made. In both instances resilience is impaired and stress is born.

The result is that we begin to feel we have all kinds of ills. The slightest touch of indigestion becomes heart-disease and the tiniest lump on the surface of the skin is cancer! We are often too afraid to go to the doctor lest he confirm our worst suspicions.

Stress arising from either of these causes threatens many of us. We are prisoners of the very inventions we created to make life easier. Year by year we have to live faster and faster to keep up with their demands. No wonder businessmen call it the rat-race!

But perhaps the hardest forms of stress are those concerned with human relationships. We have considered the stress of grief arising from bereavement; but other sad estrangements can happen. I think, for example, of the grief of a parent as he sees his beloved child go out into the wilderness and become lost. There are so many parents whose sons or daughters have left home and are now drifting with the drug-sampling drop-outs of our world. The parable of the prodigal son who breaks the heart of his father is as real as it was on the day that Jesus told it.

Is it not again just here that we find there is Someone who understands? For Jesus allowed Himself to be stretched to the limit, too, in His infinite love for us. In the Garden of Gethsemane, all the sin and sickness of the world pressing upon Him, His heart was breaking to bring us healing and peace. He found Himself majestically alone knowing that the only way forward lay through the insults, the whips, the thorns and the cross.

But Jesus went not only to the limit. Where you or I would have cracked under the strain He continued to bear the full weight of the world's sufferings, refusing even the solace of wine. For Him there was no escape. To complete the work of our salvation-wholeness He had to go on to the end. Only so could He be the captain of every man's salvation and only so could the works of God be released in our midst.

What can we do if stress comes? The art of relaxation is helpful but it is not so easy to find peace by leaning back in an armchair or by going for long walks. Still the mind races round and round and we find it difficult to keep our emotions under control.

One positive thing we can do is to try concentrating on the five senses God has given us. If we go for a walk we can look more carefully than we have done before at the beauty around us. It has shapes and colours that perhaps we had forgotten, and there are sounds and fragrances, too. Probably, when we were children, we knew what it was like to lie in the grass, watching the movement of the trees in the wind and hearing the song of the birds. Life was good, then, and there was plenty of time. We can try being children like this all over again. Most of us still have the five good gifts of taste, smell, touch, hearing and sight. We can exercise them again. It may be that God can use the simple wild flower growing in the hedgerow as a sacrament of His healing touch.

I remember, when I was going through such a difficult period, motoring to the sea. I was vaguely conscious, as I clambered down the steps from the promenade, of a few other people. I walked along the sand for a little while and then sat down on a ridge of pebbles heaped up by the tide. As I did so a shell at my side drew my attention. Its colours were beautiful and deep and as I turned it slowly in my hand they melted into one another and sometimes changed their shade. There were probably many other shells nearby but this one seemed to speak to me in a language deeper than words. It seemed to contain all the beauty and peace of the universe. I could not put it down and I stayed sitting there for two hours or more. In that shell I found renewed strength. Not a strength, perhaps, that would last for ever, though I remember it as clearly as though it were only yesterday. In the hours and days that followed I thanked God for it. It was such a simple thing, yet it conveyed an infinity of love and peace.

It is important not so much to turn away from a situation that hurts as to turn to something that completely holds our whole attention. The only way to empty one's mind of one set of thoughts is to fill it with another.

Michael was a young curate who had come almost straight from university and theological college, bursting with enthusiasm, into a highly respectable parish. He was going to turn the world upside down but, unhappily, it did just that to him. In the middle of his second year he was near to a nervous breakdown. His vicar telephoned me to ask if I could help. I had met Michael earlier and had thought he would do a splendid job in his ministry. When I called to see him I was sorry to find him in a very dejected state. He told me he had lost all his faith.

It is never easy for a newly ordained man, specially if he has had little experience of the world, to adjust himself to the new way in which people look at him. As soon as he arrives, a stranger among a mass of strange people, and puts his collar on backwards, he is expected to become something he has never been before. The parish expects him to conform to a certain image that has been built up about what a curate should be. To please, he tries to adjust himself to it. For Michael, the struggle had been too hard. Had he gone to a working-class parish, where folk accept you just as you are, it might have been easier for him, but this one was riddled with respectability and tradition.

There was not much I could do but listen on that first

occasion, but I did manage to let him see that in trying to be somebody else he was denying the God Who had called him. It was Michael God had chosen and ordained and not some faceless man. What he had to do was to discover himself again.

I asked him if he had any hobbies and, to my delight, he told me that he had. He used to build model aeroplanes. He went to his book-shelves and showed me books on the subject. When I left he had promised that for the next two months he would leave all his parish problems on one side and return to his hobby. His vicar was glad to co-operate. For two months he would not ask Michael to preach and would let him find his own way.

I called on him again during this period and found his study strewn with diagrams, balsa wood, string and glue. Already he had made three splendid models and was starting on a fourth. But what pleased me most was that the Michael I had known was coming back again.

Sometimes we have to stop striving and allow God to come to us in His own time and in His own way. Michael was doing this now. He completed his curacy there and has long since become a much beloved vicar in another town. He is married and has three delightful children. He still has his enthusiasm but to it has been added a depth of understanding and patience that he hadn't had before. He realises that he doesn't have to play a part. God, who designed and made each one of us, can use him just as he is.

The worst thing about stress is that it throws everything out of perspective. It magnifies the ego and exaggerates every slightest hurt. In this condition even the normal flow of nature's healing energies is blocked and the work that God wants to do in us is inhibited. It is not that He no longer cares or wants to heal us. On the contrary, His heart goes out to us all the more. Is there anything we can do at these times that will enable us to receive the help He so freely wants to give?

When the pressures mount I lie flat on my back and, after having taken a few deep and prolonged breaths, at the same time seeing that every muscle in my body is perfectly relaxed, I enter into an attunement with all creation as it rests in God. I often do this at night before turning on to my side to sleep. It is probably the best time because everything is then still.

First, I think of the world of nature, the trees and plants, the birds and wild creatures, all now at rest, and I let myself become, with them, a part of God's total creation. Then I think of the sky, the stars and the vast distances between them, the majestic infinity of space, all held in perfect balance and design by the Originator of all things. And so I come into a realisation that all creation is in His hands. Behind this wonderful creation, yet manifest in every tiniest part of it, is the One who is eternal, without beginning and without end. I then let this realisation permeate my whole being. God becomes All in all. At this point I can let go into Him every little bit of tension within me, be it spiritual, emotional, mental or physical. I feel His cleansing and renewing energies flooding into every part of me, into the depths of my mind and memories, releasing all its anxieties and fears, and into every nerve, every cell and every tissue of my body.

Then the light of heaven, with its love and joy, ever flowing from the genesis of all creation, fills my whole being. In immediate response I find myself releasing into Him all those concerns for other people that have come my way. These are the burdens of folk who have asked me to pray for them, those I have met that day and specially any to whom I have had the privilege of ministering in our Lord's name. Often, I find that others, for no obvious and apparent reason, come into my mind and these also I let go into the moving stream of God's healing light and love. At this point one is no longer praying one's own prayers; instead one is taken up into the ceaseless creativity of God throughout the universe. One's own hopes and prayers no longer matter. Everything, just everything, is in His hands and all, therefore, is well.

I cannot describe the release and happiness that comes from doing this, but I praise God and thank Him that, through our Captain of salvation, He has made it possible.

VII

A FAITH WITHOUT LIMIT

JESUS DID NOT SEND FORTH His disciples to preach the good news of the Kingdom and to heal the sick from the seclusion of some heavenly operations-room. He was a true Captain, a Man among men, showing how it should be done and making available the power to do it. From all His disciples He chose twelve in particular that they might be with Him. As this little band accompanied Him wherever He went they were able to observe closely His healing work. They saw in Him the Supreme Instrument through whom the Kingdom of heaven breaks into the earthly scene. The time would come when they would be called to continue His work.

It is from the recorded observations of this little band, the nucleus of that family we now call the Christian church, that we who try to follow Him in our generation can learn. The Lord of us all has clearly demonstrated that His power is all about us and is available whenever, in simple obedience to His command, we set out in His name to do the work He calls us to do.

In this and the next chapter we shall be looking again at two of our Lord's healing works, and trying to see them afresh, as they saw them, while, at the same time, testing by our observation the insights He is bringing back to us.

As we have seen, Christ Himself has not changed. "He is the same yesterday, today and forever." The victory over the forces of evil has been won. "He is able to do exceeding abundantly above all that we ask or think according to the power that worketh in us" (Ephes. 3, 20).

But the Lord so often cannot do the things He would because of our lack of faith. Too often we regard the world as a hostile place where we have to wrestle for good against a God who is reluctant to give it. And too often He has to remind and reassure us, as did the father his elder son coming in from the field, "But, son, thou art ever with me, and all that I have is thine."

If, however, we who are called to follow Him have the faith it is sometimes lacking in those we would wish to help. Even the Lord cannot give to those who are not prepared to receive. To some blind men Jesus once said, "According to your faith be it done unto you." He did not say, "According to my power," or, "According to my willingness."

Faith itself does not heal. What faith does is to release the power already there and to provide a channel through which the Lord's healing energies may flow. When the channels are open His healing power can come in. And the first of the healing works we shall consider will amply illustrate this.

There was a man whose faith was so wonderfully open that the Lord "marvelled at him". He was the centurion who lived in the area of Capernaum where Jesus had done many mighty works (Luke 7, 2-10). His servant-boy, "who was dear unto him, was sick and ready to die". His request came to Jesus out of the blue and the manner in which it was made called forth from Jesus a commendation higher than that given to any other who sought His help. "I have not found so great faith," said Jesus, "no, not in Israel."

Israel, the people of faith and hope, the people God had chosen to be the instrument through which He would reveal Himself to mankind, the people to whom Jesus had been specially sent, had failed to recognise Him. It was from beyond Israel's borders that this look of recognition came. The centurion was a Roman soldier, a gentile.

There is something excitingly prophetic about the whole encounter. Matthew, in his account of the event, sees this as he goes on to record a saying of Jesus in which He speaks of those who will come from the four corners of the earth to sit down with the patriarchs in the kingdom of heaven, while those who were meant to have done will be cast out. In this encounter we see how the Lord's healing power and love reach out across all boundaries. His promises are for all. Wherever a heart is turned to Him in faith, there is the true Israel, there is the one whom the Lord can bless.

St. Luke speaks very favourably of centurions both in his gospel and in the Acts of the Apostles. Though they were officers in the army of an occupying power and would have regarded the Jewish people as being subservient to them they nevertheless showed a remarkable respect towards their religion and they were particularly responsive to the person of Jesus Himself. None more so than this one. So much did he respect their religion that he had built a synagogue for the Jews of his area and it was the elders of this synagogue who represented him to Jesus with the words, "He is worthy."

His faith would have put to shame the faith of many of us today. He had no doubt whatever that Jesus could and would willingly do the work of healing that he was asking Him to do. But how often in our day do we pray expectantly for the healing of a sufferer who is beyond the reach of medical help? How often do we protect ourselves by hiding beneath the prevailing unfaith of those around us?

Sooner or later we are brought face to face with situations that seem beyond all reasonable hope. I remember years ago having been confronted by a man who was very seriously ill with cancer. The thought passed through my mind, "Is divine healing thus far but no farther? Have I reached the boundary here?" I do not remember the exact outcome but I am glad that I ministered to him nonetheless. I know that the Lord mightily blessed him. Somehow, one has to break through the barrier of human doubt and go on ministering to such people, conscious that the healing grace of our Lord is flowing through them. The issue must be left in His hands. The wonderful thing is that when we do this there are often such changes in the situation that it is obvious that a higher power has broken in. We have a long way to go as we follow in our Lord's healing steps, but He is giving us sufficient "signs" along the path to indicate what might lie ahead. When His whole body becomes united in the faith that all things are possible we shall see the "mightier works" that He promised.

Turning again to the centurion, there are three important facets to his faith that are well worth considering in more detail. First, his clear recognition of the authority Jesus possessed. Secondly, his realisation that Jesus could use the faith of one on behalf of another. Thirdly, that Jesus could heal at a distance.

The centurion would certainly have heard many reports of the healing work Jesus had done in the neighbourhood; he may, indeed, have witnessed some of them. What he had heard and perhaps seen must have deeply impressed him. Authority was something that he knew and could recognise. It was this note in the character of Jesus that had so struck the local populace when He first visited the synagogue there. It was with authority that Jesus preached and with authority that He cast out an unclean spirit.

Behind the centurion lay the power of the Roman Empire. The orders that he issued to his subordinates were not just of his own making. The stamp of Caesar was upon them. In watching Jesus he knew that here was another who was also under authority. In that sense he was a kindred spirit. But the power behind Jesus and that worked through Him was on a different and higher plane altogether. While the Jews were arguing among themselves by what authority Jesus did these things, the centurion instinctively knew and was deeply humbled and impressed.

It was this humility that prompted him to ask the elders to present his case, rather than appear personally. And Jesus, accompanied by them, set out immediately to the centurion's home in response. But they had not gone far before the centurion, hearing that Jesus was on His way, sent another message and it was this that drew from Jesus such a high commendation of his faith.

"Lord, trouble not thyself: for I am not worthy that thou shouldest enter under my roof . . . But say in a word, and my servant shall be healed. For I also am a man set under authority . . . and I say unto one, Go, and he goeth: and to another, Come, and he cometh; and to my servant, Do this, and he doeth it."

So, again are we reminded of the divine authority

implicit in our healing work for the Kingdom, an authority that intertwines with compassion and love. The keynotes of our work are awareness and obedience —awareness to the movement of the Holy Spirit whenever we are faced by someone in need, awareness of what God is already saying in that situation and, finally, an awareness of what He wants us to do in it. Behind us is the whole power of the Kingdom. Our orders on what we are to say and to do come from above and to them we must respond obediently.

Let us consider the centurion's realisation that Jesus could use the faith of one on behalf of another. He was making what we would call an act of intercession. What lifted it above the level of many such acts was its inherent sense of expectancy.

Intercession seems to be particularly valid when there is a bond of identification between the sufferer and the one who intercedes. If both are members of the same family and household, as in this case, the bond is already there. They are part of each other's being. Jesus accepts the faith of one and uses it as a channel of healing for the other.

In most instances when we intercede it is for someone not already close to us, often a stranger who turns to us for help and asks us to pray on his or her behalf. The request may come out of the blue. I always think that such requests are already proceeding to the throne of grace and that what we are being asked to do is to help them on their way. When I receive such a request, usually by post, I take the letter in both hands and try to get the "feel" of the sender and of the situation he was in at the moment he wrote it. I try to take into my own being something of the hurt he was feeling. Then I lift the letter between my hands upwards and offer the burden it contains immediately into the presence of our healing Lord. I deal with it there and then. At the close of the day, when entering into attunement with the whole of creation and with the eternal Source of all things, I finally relinquish that burden, together with all the others that have come my way, into the ceaseless movement of God's healing love. There, after having held those burdens in a spirit of complete and loving surrender and feeling them released into His hands, I leave them with a "Thank you, Lord".

The thanksgiving at the end and its reiteration in the following days whenever the thought of that person comes into mind is important because it helps us to realise that the burden is now with the Lord. Once it has been handed over it must be left there. We must not take it back in order to go through the whole process again. The Lord cannot set into motion forces to bring healing into that situation until we hand the reins completely over to Him.

This handing over in complete trust is not always easy. I think of those relationships where there are deep emotional ties. There is the anxious concern of the mother for the sickness of her child, of the husband for his wife, of someone for his dearest friend. It would be easier for them if Christ were still among us in the flesh, and they could see Him and touch Him. For such as these I can think of nothing better than their sharing with a Christian friend, with a priest or minister or with a prayer group.

The faith of the centurion was such that he instinctively knew that Jesus could heal at a distance. This was remarkable because at that time it was commonly believed that Jesus, like any other healer, would have to be actually present with the sufferer in order to heal him. It was thought that healing could be conveyed only by touch. In his own faith the centurion was unconsciously presaging the Easter promise of our Lord that wherever we might be and in whatever age we might live, His presence would be with us.

Another gentile, a Syrophoenician woman, was similarly convinced of healing at a distance. Her daughter lay ill at home and in her plea to Jesus for His healing touch she did not ask Him to go to her house. Her persistent faith again elicited from Jesus a high commendation. "O woman," He said, "great is thy faith; be it unto thee even as thou wilt" (Mark 7, 24-30).

It is on the basis of such healing incidents* that we sometimes use what we call absent or distant healing. It is different from intercession in that its movement is outward rather than upward. In intercession we take the weight of the sufferer and lift him, as it were, upwards into the presence of the risen Christ. In absent healing we begin by becoming clothed about with the divine presence and then we go out in spirit to where the sufferer is.

Absent healing begins only after we have first become established in the heavenlies. This is vitally important. If it were otherwise it would simply be an attempt at psychic healing. After all the preliminaries of prayer are over, when confession, thanksgiving and petition have been made and we enter into the unseen realm of God's perfect kingdom to dwell in silent conversation with

*I am accepting the usual assumption that the healing of the nobleman's son (John 4, 46-53) is another version of the same story. Here, whether it is or not, the point remains the same and is even more dramatic.

Him, then it is we can begin. While still dwelling in the heavenlies we go out, as it were, to the room where our sick friend lies. Conscious of the Lord's presence and His light and joy filling us, we minister to him there.

Sometimes I go on to minister to others. As in other times of prayer, I find that after having ministered in this way to those in special need, others are brought into awareness, and I minister to them, too.

Inevitably this leads to a joyful identification with the never-ending flow of God's purifying and healing Love as it is outpoured upon all creation from the throne of grace. At this point comes a glimpse of the world as it might be, as Jesus saw it when He was on earth and as He still sees it now. He looks, through the eyes of God, upon everything that He has made and, behold! it is very good.

We are learning much today about telepathy. Scientists have proved that extra-sensory perception exists, and that distance is of no account. I believe that the highest manifestation of this mysterious phenomenon, and the reason why God has given it, is to be found in the practice of distant healing.

Telepathy's part in prayer works both ways. Sometimes we receive a message through the ether from someone of whom perhaps we have not heard for a long time. Often it is followed by news of them, or a communication from them, a few days later. When this happens to me I always lift up in prayer the person who has so unexpectedly come into my mind and, in the Lord Christ's name, I send a blessing out to them. Sometimes, after having prayed for others, either in intercession or absent healing, we hear they felt a wonderful peace surrounding and filling them. Some speak of a "glow of warmth" or a "presence of light", and it is a lovely thing to discover that this happened to them at the time when prayer was being made.

When a priest or minister raises his hand in blessing, something more than a pious hope is being expressed. He is actively conveying, by divine authority, an effective means of grace. He is allowing himself to be used as a channel of the creative energies of God flowing through him for the healing and strengthening of his people. I remember how a leading industrialist once said to me, immediately following a service in which a well-loved bishop gave the blessing, "When that man gives his blessing you can feel it. It fills the atmosphere of the whole church."

Absent healing is like that. It can be used by any Christian believer at the point of prayer when he knows he is "in Christ". Thus he identifies himself with the Lord's outgoing care and compassion for all who suffer.

A whole congregation can use this method. As an alternative way of prayer to that of intercession, the leader can involve the whole body of Christ there assembled in sending out beyond the walls of the church and into the homes of the parish where sick ones lie, and into the families where there is disarray, the blessing of Christ's healing power and love. This they do in His name. Then, after a moment or two of silence, the amens of the congregation are added.

I like the way Camps Farthest Out do this. They invariably bring into their worship a time when, clothed about with the risen Lord, they face each point of the compass in turn. Then they hold out their arms and hands in blessing towards the countries they face. There is something more mysteriously wonderful than mere symbolism here as they send blessings of Christ-filled love to the peoples of Russia and China, to those of America and to the rest of the globe.

One of my American friends tells me that when she travels by coach, train or plane she sends out a blessing to the crew and to her fellow-passengers. She projects the spirit of divine love to each of them in turn. I have sometimes done this myself and have no doubt about its effect.

Distance, as the centurion instinctively knew, makes no difference in the realm of Christ's healing love. However far away a friend may be, he is close when we are in Christ. The Lord uses our faith as we abide in Him as the channel through which His power and healing love can flow.

VIII

AS A GRAIN OF MUSTARD SEED

NOW LET US TURN from one end of the scale to another, from the high level of faith that we saw in the centurion to one far more simple. It is that of the poor woman who, in her ignorance, tried to take the healing virtue from our Lord by secretly touching the hem of His garment. Her need was great. "She had an issue of blood twelve years, and had suffered many things of many physicians, and had spent all that she had, and was nothing bettered, but rather grew worse" (Mark 5, 25-34).

It is a story in two parts. Had she been able to do what she set out to do it would have ended half-way and we would probably never have heard of her. But it did not end there. Though she was able to fulfil her ambition she had not reckoned on what it would do to Jesus and the response it would evoke from Him. There is a cost in healing. It is not by the waving of a magic wand but "by his stripes (that) we are healed". In the moment that she came close enough to touch Him He felt the virtue going out of Him and immediately knew there was someone there in desperate need.

She was a lonely woman and would have talked much with herself. Over and over again she kept telling herself, "If I can touch but His clothes I shall be whole." She had no one to tell her how exactly healing happened. All she knew was that in Jesus there was a power to heal. It seemed reasonable to her simple mind that if others were set free from their troubles just by the touch of His hand, all she need do was to get close enough to touch Him and the power would flow into her. Even to touch His clothes would be enough. He need not know what she was doing. She would wait till an opportunity came. One day, it did.

The quality of her faith hardly seemed to be of the kind we would normally recommend sufferers to have today! It almost borders on the superstitious and many, had it happened in this more enlightened age, would have questioned its validity. They would have tried to get her to change her ideas. Yet the Lord used her simple faith just as it was. It was good enough for Him.

One of the surprising things about this ministry is that it often seems to be those who are on or beyond the fringe of the orthodox Christian church, and who have little understanding of what we really believe, who are most readily and powerfully blessed. The energies of our Lord's healing grace have no limits, no boundary. No matter how apparently poor the quality of faith, how strange their ideas about Christian belief, if it is real and sincere in its own right, the Lord will use it.

I have often been asked to put my hand on the back of someone just passing by. Sometimes it may be the joint of a limb or some other part of the body. There was a time when I would hesitate to do this without first sitting down with the sufferer and asking what it was all about. I would want to know something of his faith. But I have done what I have been asked and invariably the pain or tenseness has diminished or gone.

Occasionally, clergy are asked to bless a cross that someone has bought to wear and, at other times, perhaps to send a handkerchief which has been blessed for their healing or for the healing of a loved one. If they are anything like me they experience a fleeting moment of questioning in their minds as to whether or not this is superstition. But, after that moment has passed, I have always done what they have asked me to do and have never found it has hindered them in their search for God but rather the contrary. One is comforted by the fact that even St. Paul did not refuse this kind of action! (Acts 19, 12).

The spiritual laws operating in this field can be only dimly understood, but perhaps one might make two comments. I put them in the form of questions because they are more for discussion than intended as definitive statements.

First, how far have we become indoctrinated by a formal Christianity that has little or no room for the supernatural? In place of the risks and uncertainty of a living faith in One who can turn the expected into the unexpected how far do we prefer to have a religion that simply brings us comfort and the spiritual uplift we need to live good lives? It is not easy to launch out into the deeps. We do not want to get lost. We want to know just where we are. Miracles are happenings we cannot explain. If we hear a preacher telling us that the healing works of Jesus are to be taken not literally but spiritually, we feel safe. When he explains that when Jesus makes the blind to see, it is the eyes of our spiritual understanding that is meant, we are content. That is a message our minds can accept.

It is a remarkable thing that we cannot pray for miracles to happen with the same confidence and expectancy as did the early church. We have become inhibited. During the centuries between, our attitude has changed. We are quite happy to pray for the sick, and it gives us a warm feeling when we do, but we are not at all sure that it is God's will that we should pray for their healing. We have long grown used to the illogicality of suggesting that He wants us to carry our sicknesses in the spirit of cross-bearing while not objecting if the doctor takes that opportunity away!

Secondly, is this work of healing more evangelistic than pastoral in its nature? Has it more to do with the frontiers of the Kingdom's advance than the strengthening of its base? Our Lord linked it with the proclamation of the gospel and promised His disciples that as they went forth to preach the Kingdom their preaching would be accompanied with "signs following". When previously He had sent them out on a training mission He seemed to identify the healing work they would do as a sign that the Kingdom was nigh. Later, when the infant church was being persecuted in Jerusalem following the healing of the lame beggar at the Beautiful Gate of the temple its members met together and prayed for such signs to be given:

"And now, Lord, behold their threatenings, and grant unto thy servants, that with all boldness they may speak thy word, by stretching forth thy hand to heal; and that signs and wonders may be done by the name of thy holy child, Jesus" (Acts 4, 29-30).

Clearly, the early Christians identified the work of healing with that of its out-going witness to the gospel. It was a mark of the new age and was as natural a consequence of the spread of God's Kingdom as is fruit to the tree.

This is not, of course, to say that our Lord's healing

grace is denied to the faithful members of His own body. On the contrary. Many of us have experienced and continue to experience the flow of His healing and releasing power in our midst. In the heart of our worship, our times of prayer together, and in the sacraments, healing is to be found. But if there is any truth in the observation I have just made, and I believe there is, are we not neglecting one of the most important weapons in our evangelistic advance?

I cannot resist adding that if it is at the frontiers of our life in the Kingdom that its works are most clearly and dramatically to be seen, it seems poetic and even prophetic that it was but the hem of His garment that this poor woman touched!

When she did so she knew immediately that what she had hoped and expected to happen had happened! "Straightway, the fountain of her blood was dried up; and she felt in her body that she was healed of that plague." Her illness was cured at last. Had her story ended here she would have returned home, her mission fulfilled. She would have been numbered among the many thousands who have received the healing touch of our Lord, and whose stories never have and never will be told.

But the story does not end here. At this point the second half begins and it is more wonderful than the first.

Feeling that some of life's energy had gone out of Him, Jesus called out, "Who touched me?" We can imagine the scene. He was hurrying to the bedside of a dying child and a great crowd was with Him. People were pressing on Him from all sides. It was a strange question to ask, thought the disciples. "Thou seest the multitude thronging thee, and sayest thou, Who touched me?" they said. But Jesus knew that the one who had done so would know what He meant. Someone in that great crowd had touched Him with special intent. This was what made all the difference. Being what He was, the captain of our salvation-wholeness and not just a natural healer, He had to stop in His tracks to find out exactly who this person was.

One of those phrases most of us dislike to hear is, "I didn't bother you because you were too busy." This could never be used of Jesus. Though His ministry among us was only three years, and though, during that short time, He changed the whole pattern and course of history, He was never too busy for any man. And now this woman became the focal point of all His attention.

As he turned round to see who it was who had touched Him, there she was, falling down on her knees at His feet and telling Him "all the truth". Other translations put it, "the whole truth". I often wonder what she told Him. No record is kept beyond the few details we are told. With this kind of illness she would have been regarded as an unclean person with whom no ordinary decent folk would mix. Did she tell Him how lonely she had been? Did she tell Him of the hopelessness and bitterness that had come to fill her heart, perhaps even of resentment against life and against the God who made it, for having been treated so? She had spent every penny that she had. Did she tell Him of her deep anxieties and fears about what lay in the future? It seems likely that she did. She poured it all out and Jesus, supreme in His understanding and compassion, listened to every word.

His reply was immediate and to her it must have been

the most wonderful reply in all the world. It was exceeding abundantly above all she might have asked or thought possible.

It began with Jesus calling her "daughter"! This was a name she had probably not heard addressed to her since childhood. Possibly she might have been known by other names, but never this one. She had come seeking a magical cure; she had found a person who perfectly understood. In Jesus she had met someone who cared, someone with whom there was a personal relationship.

For healing is not just the lifting of a hurt from our minds and bodies. It goes deeper than that. It is concerned not only with the present illness; it also has to do with the deeper levels of our sickness. What brings us to seek His help in the first place may well be some immediate and obvious need, but in His presence we come to realise there are other, more underlying, needs within. Under His penetrating yet understanding gaze we know that it is the bitterness, the resentments we have long cherished, the fears and the guilts that most need the touch of His healing grace. We then realise that the work of healing is ultimately a matter of relationship with a person, with Jesus Himself.

"Daughter," said Jesus to her, "thy faith hath made thee whole."

Her faith, so poor and pitiful, had brought her a long way. She had sought a cure; she had found wholeness. What a world of difference there is between the two! It is unfortunate that some of our modern translations blur this important point. There is a similar use of these contrasting words in the story of the ten lepers. All were cured—or cleansed—of their illness. Only the one who returned to give thanks was made whole.

We can be sure that the underlying meaning of this phrase, together with that which immediately followed it, would not be lost on those who were crowding round. They yearned for a Messiah, a captain of salvation who would lead them out of bondage and into salvation-wholeness. This Jesus was He, and this woman's simple faith had led her to Him.

"Go into peace," He added to her. It meant more than simply, "Go in peace." The phrase had its own significance. It spoke of the Jews' long cherished hope for a land of freedom, health and prosperity. All these shades of meaning were gathered into the one word, peace. "Shalom" was what they called it. It was the heart's desire of every Jew, as it still is today. To greet a friend with the word "Shalom" was to express the deep and prayerful hope that he might be freed from bondage and that a land of peace and plenty would open to him. To this poor woman the words she heard would contain the promise of a new and wonderful life. "Daughter, thy faith hath made thee whole, go into peace."

The Lord accepts people just as they are and He meets them at the point of their need. However untutored their faith may be, if it is real and sincere, He uses it as a channel for His healing and renewing power. Be it only as a grain of mustard seed, it is big enough for Him.

IX

THE AWAKENING OF FAITH

FAITH IS A QUALITY latent in every one. We cannot create it ourselves, nor can we, by our own efforts, enlarge it once it has been awakened. It is a response mechanism built into us by the Creator Himself and can come into being only by being evoked by someone or something outside of ourselves. It finds its true and ultimate fulfilment when we forget ourselves in completely trustful surrender to Him who is the Source of all being. When that happens the channels of our salvation-wholeness are open, and the works of God can be done in us.

There is a lovely story in the gospels showing how faith became awakened in one particular town and how it spread, like a contagion, throughout the whole district. The town was Gadara (more probably, Gergesa) and the district to which it belonged was known as Decapolis. The story might be regarded as a classic pattern of how faith can take root in any one of our modern parishes and from there spread out into the whole of the deanery to which it belongs.

As its name implies, Decapolis was a district of ten towns or villages that were originally settlements of Graeco-Roman origin. It was situated in the wild country on the eastern side of the lake and therefore quite unconnected with the area of Galilee where Jesus did most of His preaching and healing work. On three occasions Jesus passed through that way on a roundabout route to or from the northern district of Tyre, and on each of these occasions something of great significance happened.

Let us look at the story as it is unfolded in the pages of the gospels and see what we can find in it for the life of the church today. We turn, first, to Mark 5, 1-20.

The story begins with the witness of one man. Sometimes we use the phrase "healed to serve", and it was certainly true of him. He told his friends of what great things the Lord had done for him and throughout Decapolis the news of his remarkable healing spread. When all is said and done, what makes Christian faith infectious is news, not views. No argument can stand in the face of obvious fact, as when the man who had been born blind came face to face with Jesus. It did not matter how much the religious leaders argued about it, the plain and inescapable fact remained. "One thing I know," he told them, "whereas I was blind, now I see."

The man from Gadara had been possessed by devils. Most of the time he had spent among the hills and in and around the caves where the townsfolk buried their dead. Here he would scream aloud in his torment, trying to cut the devils out of himself with sharp stones. Often such friends as he had would try to restrain him, binding him with chains and fetters, but he had always burst them apart. This part of his story they would know better than he, and specially those who had young children to protect. But to the poor man himself those days would now soon be forgotten. Already they were becoming only a dim shadow in his memory, like a bad dream from which he was awakening.

The first his befuddled mind would have known of it

was when he had felt something wonderful happening to him (Jesus was casting the evil spirit out of him) and he was being asked his name. Using the only one he knew, whether it had been coined by himself or by his friends, he had replied, "Legion; for we are many."

He would never forget the questioner. The men who were with Him had called Him "Master", and immediately he had known why. Here was someone who was not afraid of him. Though His eyes were full of an understanding and compassion he had never seen before, there was also an authority about Him that was undeniable. In His presence he felt safe.

He wanted to stay with Jesus, to join the band of men who accompanied Him and to go with them on their journey. But, to his disappointment, the Master would not allow it. Instead, He told him, "Go home to thy friends, and tell them how great things the Lord hath done for thee and hath had compassion on thee." At least, the Master had given him something positive to do, and he would do it. In Jewry itself, Jesus always instructed those whom He healed to go quietly and to tell no one, but this was gentile land.

We can imagine how the man set out to fulfil his task. He would have found, to his consternation, that there was opposition. He had not realised that while he was experiencing his first taste of freedom from the bondage that had imprisoned him his townsfolk were remonstrating with Jesus, praying Him to depart out of their coasts. They did not want Him there. Legion would have been nonplussed by their attitude. But it has often happened that way. Folk do not want to be disturbed. They prefer to stay as they are. To admit the presence of Jesus into a situation in all His fullness, as healer as well as teacher, is sometimes too uncomfortable a challenge.

But Legion persisted. He could not have helped it if he had tried. He had met the most wonderful person in the world. That was what he knew and what he wanted everybody to know. If Jesus had changed his life, what could He not do in the lives of others? If Jesus had released him from such a terrible bondage, could there be any destroying power of sin or sickness that He could not heal?

I have known many a congregation and many a deanery having to change its thinking about the healing ministry because of the witness of one man or one woman whose life has been changed by the touch of the living Christ. The consciousness of another dimension has entered in. Out of that witness has been born the beginnings of a new and deeper understanding of what the power of a full gospel can do.

The story of this man's healing is a remarkable one. There exists no other account of an exorcism more dramatic than this, and no other so descriptive, at the same time, of our Lord's perfect understanding and compassion. It is a classic.

We are thinking more about possession and exorcism—the ministry of deliverance—in these days. I remember not so long ago when we thought of these things as having no place in this enlightened age. They belonged to the pages of the Bible. The nearest we got to the subject was when we listened to the stories brought home by our missionaries from countries far away. What they told us was fascinating but hard to believe. They spoke about whole areas that seemed to possess an evil atmosphere, of individuals who had come under the dominion of dark powers. Their stories seemed barely credible.

But, now, whether the academics agree or not, things have changed. We find ourselves in a new age of permissiveness where the guarding restraints of a pervading Christian faith are being thrown overboard. The result is that evil powers have free play and the need for the ministry of deliverance is increasing.

Too often do our clergy find themselves confronted by situations where either people or places need releasing from the presence of dominating evil powers. It is our young people who suffer most. Enjoying the new-found freedom we have given them, they experiment in spheres from which they ought to have been protected. Some, perhaps more psychically sensitive and not so emotionally secure as others, seek a thrill by engaging in a deep form of mind-emptying meditation, sometimes aided by drugs, in which no attempt at all is made to guard the door against the possibility of evil forces coming in. Others, led by dare-devils—an appropriate name!—get hurt through going to parties where the ouija board is used or some other attempt is made to get into touch with outside presences. Others, yet again, try to learn and use witchcraft. Their efforts to find complete freedom lead them inexorably towards a terrible bondage.

But it is not only through experimentation in the psychic realm that the gate of the mind can open to incoming forces of evil. A person can also nurture a resentment so bitter that it spurns the offer of forgiveness, a grief so deep that it refuses to be comforted, a state of jealousy so consuming that it will not be checked. Eventually an evil power enters into the personality and takes over its control. Only a ministry of release in the name of Christ can then set him free.

Much is being said by the media about exorcism and a misleading and horrific impression is being created. While evil is, beyond doubt, evil, and much is made of that, it is nothing compared to the much more impressive power of good. There is an overriding movement of love and compassion that envelops such a ministration when it is given by the authority and in the name of Jesus. Exorcisms are dramatic, but not in the way the media popularly supposes them to be. What is in fact memorable about them is the atmosphere of joy and release and the sense of praise.

I remember having been told, when I was the resident chaplain of a leading psychiatric hospital, that a newly admitted young man was calling for me. When I saw him, he told me that he was possessed and that he wanted me to drive the devil out of him. Though I had sometimes heard of this kind of thing before, there was something different about this one. I knew that I could not leave him without acceding to his request. So, as he lay there in his bed, in the holy name of Jesus I commanded the unclean spirit to come out of him. Immediately, he went into a kind of paroxysm, the upper part of his body, jack-knifing at the hips, rose as though some great force had suddenly thrown him, and his forehead hit his feet. Till then he had been lying still, surrendering himself to what he possibly thought was to have been simply a prayer about to be offered for him. Obviously, he was not expecting anything more, neither was I! Two or three times in quick succession these apparently uncontrollable spasms happened and then, suddenly, it was all over. As he lay there he sighed deeply, smiled at me and held out his hand. I took it in mine and sat down at his side. I prayed inwardly, for there was perfect silence between us, that the Spirit of God would flood his whole being with peace. After a while I left him.

In the afternoon I returned to see how he was but could not find him. I made enquiries and discovered, to my sorrow, that shortly after I had left him he had been wheeled into another room to receive electro-convulsant therapy. Not, as I believed, that he now needed it, but simply because his turn for treatment had arrived. He was next on the list. I deeply regretted that there had been no opportunity to tell his doctor, who was a friend of mine, what had happened. The doctor was busy with treatments that day and immediately after having ministered to the young man I, on my part, had had to go to the hospital chapel to conduct services.

It is a memory that still stands clearly in my mind. I believe that in that morning's ministration the young man had been perfectly released and healed. Later that evening I was able to tell the doctor about it and the young man received no more treatment. He later came to me to express his gratitude. Though little was said it was obvious that he knew something had happened to him that he could not explain. He returned home very happily.

My experience since those days when I was a chaplain, and therefore no longer constrained by loyalty to the hospital system, has been to find that some who would normally have been admitted for psychiatric treatment have benefited instead from the ministry of deliverance performed in our Lord's name. This has been particularly so with sufferers from depressive disorders. Many such patients can be treated outside hospital today as there are new medicaments now available to the general practitioner. These, it seems to me, "bind" the illness without necessarily casting it out. But we can thank God that these treatments, at least, do this. Any further treatment at a deeper level ought to come from that divine authority and power which Christ has committed to His church.

There are far more patients having to rely on these modern drugs than there ought to be. The doctors are doing a wonderful job trying to cope with them all. In many instances they are filling the gaps that we have left. Perhaps they are giving us time to catch up.

I met a young man, barely out of his teens, suffering from depression. He had found shelter with a London vicar whose door is always open to those who have lost their way in life. He had been to a doctor and told me of the drug he had been given. Though given compassionately, it would not do more than "bind" the illness and so enable him to live with it. I felt that something more was needed. The vicar and three of his workers joined me in prayer for his release and there and then we rebuked his spirit of depression. In the name of Jesus we commanded it to loose its hold. I then put my hands upon his head while we prayed the Holy Spirit to fill him in every part of his being, body, mind and soul. He slumped forward in his chair. After a moment we helped him to his feet and he went upstairs to bed. Hardly had he thrown himself down on it than he fell into a deep and refreshing sleep. When he returned there was really no need for him to tell us, though he did, that he felt a different person!

I have written about the three levels of sickness: that

of the illness itself; the level where its predisposing causes are to be found; and finally, the third level in which lies the deep stratum of evil consequent upon the fall.

As I become aware of the deepest level I often wonder how far some of our mentally very sick are affected by elemental forces of evil, by our adversary the devil who "as a roaring lion, walketh about seeking whom he may devour" (1 Peter, 5, 8). Psychiatry has to do with the first and second levels, but some of my psychiatrist friends appreciate that the depth of human life does not end there. Occasionally they see patients who cannot easily and satisfactorily be classified in purely psychological terms.

It is not always only the illness that needs to be healed; it is the man himself. There are those who enjoy ill health. Their troubles are like protective clothes without which they would feel naked and exposed. Something at the very core of their being is terribly sick. To give them medicines is the most compassionate thing a doctor can do, and a clergyman by his constant visits shows at least that he cares. But neither is really satisfied. Both are aware that such help is only transitory and little more than a holding exercise. It is the psyche that really needs to be healed.

Somewhere within every man there is a kind of mechanism that regulates his whole life, his health, his desires or lack of them, and his attitude to his fellow men. This mechanism swings like a metronome from one extreme to the other. At one extreme it points to the "death wish" and, at the other, to "the strong will to live". For most of us it stays mostly somewhere in the middle, near the norm. But occasionally, when we are suddenly hit by grief or any other great shock, it clings for a while to the negative side. With some it stays there.

There was a man who for many years lived in a wheelchair. His home contained everything to make it as easy as possible for him to fend for himself. He went to a service of healing and, during the ministration, felt as if there were an electric current flowing through him. He was completely shaken. After the service he asked himself what he was doing in that chair. He got up and walked. He is now completely free.

I talked with his doctor, who first broached the subject to me, about what had happened. We had met in the house of a mutual friend. He told me that he and his colleagues had done all they could for the man and could find nothing basically wrong with him. It had puzzled them all along. His nervous system seemed to be in good fettle, his muscles, though wasted, still sound. But there was something they could not find that was holding him back. We agreed that here was a perfect healing of the man's psyche.

I remember a young woman who had been completely healed from one of the most stubborn diseases of all, disseminated sclerosis, and who came to be used in the healing ministry. It was Godfrey Mowatt who had ministered to her. When he laid his hands upon her head in Christ's name she became aware of a *terrifying* realisation of God's holiness. We were at a meeting where a number of people engaged in the healing ministry were sharing some of their experiences. Suddenly she turned to me and said, "George, these people talk about healing as though it were a lovely thing. To me it was an awe-ful experience."

I suppose that to have one's whole life changed can be

a shattering experience. When it is the psyche that has been "bound" perhaps shattering is the right word!

It is significant that during the whole of the encounter between Jesus and Legion at the lakeside there is no mention of the sufferer's prior need for faith. As with the healing of the woman bound by a "spirit of infirmity" that we considered earlier, the entire initiative is taken by Jesus Himself. The healing of Legion, as with her, springs solely from the Lord's own supreme command of the situation.

So are we reminded that, if we are to follow in His steps, the initiative rests with us who represent Him. To insist that a sufferer must have faith before we can minister to him is not New Testament teaching. To try to urge him into faith can be harmful. Jesus puts the onus of faith on His followers when He says, "he that believes shall lay hands on the sick." He did not say, "he shall lay hands on him who believes."

When, along with the divine authority committed to us, we accept the onus of faith in ministering to a sufferer, we invariably find that his own capacity for faith is awakened as a consequence. Later, he often speaks of the experience as something wonderful that happened to him in that moment. Life, for him, began to take on a new look. No longer did he feel bound by the spirit of sickness. He began to realise the glorious divine presence.

This sense of the divine presence came to Legion, and began to grow in him when he encountered Jesus on the shores of Decapolis. He would remember this more than anything else. He was a changed man living in a new environment, the environment of the Kingdom. The nightmare of his days and nights among the tombs and in the wild hills belonged to the past. In Jesus he had met someone who had changed his life, someone who had understood his condition without being afraid of it. In Jesus he had met a love and compassion that no other man had ever shown him before.

As he went out and published abroad to the people living in the ten towns what great things the Lord had done for him, his own story would soon have dispersed their fears. Their original hostility towards Jesus would have given way to a desire to see Him again. As they listened to the witness of this once-possessed man, now clothed and in his right mind, and could see for themselves what Jesus had done for him, then "all men did marvel".

It needs only a little effort to imagine the ultimate effect that the first visit of Jesus to the deanery of Decapolis had on the minds and hearts of the people there. Certainly His second and third visits were so different, but these we shall consider in our next chapter.

X

THE SPREADING OF FAITH

THE SECOND TIME Jesus visited the shores of Decapolis a crowd came to greet Him. Leading them was a little group who brought to Him "one that was deaf, and had an impediment in his speech; and they beseech him to put his hand upon him" (Mark 7, 31-37).

It was not that he was dumb. Having presumably been born deaf, he would have no idea of sound. All he knew was that by opening their mouths and manipulating throat and breathing, people made something communicable happen. When he tried it, only uncouth sounds came.

No doubt he was looked upon as an object of pity. Children would have teased him and laughed at him and possibly he was regarded as the village fool. I remember my first encounter with such a man when I was a boy. He was the youngest son of our headmaster and not much older than us boys. Like Legion in the wild hills he seemed to spend most of his time in a corner of the paddock at the back of the school where there were great heaps of garden refuse and fallen trees. That is where we invariably found him. I am afraid we used to tease him unmercifully. Perhaps it was a fear of the unknown and this was our childish way of trying to cope with it. We were too young to realise how cruel we were being. Looking back on it now, I find myself glad to remember that he got his revenge! The school was at Birkdale and every Sunday afternoon we were taken for a walk to the sandhills. There he would catch the worst offenders, pin them to the ground, and stuff their mouths full of sand. Once it happened to me. It was enough.

It was such a man they brought to Jesus. Their original hostility had long since departed. Legion's witness had borne its fruit. His faith had spread throughout the region and now they welcomed Jesus. Their act of intercession was completely trustful. They handed over the sufferer to Him. Jesus took the man, probably by the arm or hand, and led him away from the crowd. Just the two of them were alone together.

Then followed a remarkable private interview. Unhindered by the presence of others, Jesus began immediately to enter into an I-thou relationship with him. Though no words passed between them, nevertheless a deep and understanding conversation ensued. After a little while Jesus touched his ears. We are left to imagine the man's response. He must have instinctively known that here was someone who perfectly understood, who cared and who respected him as a person. Then Jesus spat and touched his tongue. Clearly, the man had surrendered himself completely into the Lord's hand. He must have felt a bond of identification between himself and the One who was treating him. Then, finally, came the critical moment when, looking upwards to heaven and with a great gathering of power stemming from the deeps within Him, Jesus called out, "Ephphatha!" The man found he had been released. The bonds of his deafness had been burst asunder. Not only could he now hear. What was more remarkable still to someone who had never learned clear speech, he could speak plainly.

In this incident we see illustrated three aspects of our ministry of healing. First, prayer groups; secondly, manual communication; thirdly, the relationship between the medical and the sacramental. Let us consider each in turn.

One of the significant marks of the recovery by the church of her healing ministry today is the formation of prayer groups everywhere. They are not organised into being; they are happenings of the Holy Spirit. Quite spontaneously one member of the Christian church invites another, perhaps two or three, to his house for praise and prayer. It needs only a few to begin with. We have our Lord's promise that where two or three are gathered together in His name, He is there in their midst. They need not be members of the same congregation or, indeed, of the same denomination. Many of these groups cut right across the barriers that divide us from one another.

I have met such groups in many different countries, and always it is the same wonderful story. Anglicans, Catholics, Lutherans, and what we in England would call the Free Churches, all are represented equally in this movement. It is the most significant part of our coming together and it is born, not of our endeavours for unity, but of the Holy Spirit.

Prayer is the seed-bed of all our healing work; indeed, of all our life and work and witness. The seed is our faith. What awakens it, nurtures it and brings it into fruition is the Holy Spirit. When that happens we rejoice in one thing only—the glory of the risen Christ; and we pray for one thing only—the coming of His

Kingdom into all creation. We bring all the sick to Him as burdens of concern. The sick situations in families and in modern society are all parts of that fallen world into which we pray that His Kingdom will come. Without prayer there is no healing.

The Lord uses faithful prayer. St. James tells us that "the prayer of faith shall save (heal) the sick" (James 5, 15). Though Jesus is always ready to take the initiative He looks for that attitude of expectant faith in our intercessory work which provides an open channel through which His power can flow. Sometimes He finds it in the sufferer himself, as in the woman who touched the hem of His garment; sometimes He finds it in someone close to the sufferer, as in a parent or the centurion who interceded on behalf of his servant-boy. Sometimes He finds it in a group whose members are in one accord as together they carry the burden of their prayer into the divine presence. In the last two of these cases faith is not necessary in the sufferer himself. Seeing the faith of the intercessor or of the group, Jesus uses it for the healing of the sick one.

We find two such groups in the gospels. The first in Capernaum, where Jesus began His public ministry and in whose region He did so many mighty works. The evangelist tells us how four men met to give of their time and energy in carrying a man sick of the palsy into the healing presence of Jesus (Mark 2, 1-12). The second is here in Decapolis, in the gentile territory across the lake, where they brought to Him the man who was deaf and had an impediment in his speech. In each case Jesus accepts the faith of the group and uses it for the healing of the sick man.

Secondly, this particular healing incident is one of

those in which we see elaborated what we would call the laying-on-of-hands. In *The Heart of Healing** I remark on the unfortunate way in which this phrase has come to have almost a technical meaning and, in some quarters, is vaguely suspect. Yet, at root, it is the simplest and most natural thing imaginable. Every parent knows what a touch can convey. Sometimes words do not go deep enough. They can even get in the way. The laying-on-of-hands is, when all is said and done, simply the healing touch of Christ.

With our Lord it was all so natural and spontaneous. When people came to Him for help He never said, "All right, first kneel down and make your confession and then I will give you the laying-on-of-hands." He simply accepted such little or great faith as they were able to bring to Him, entered into their suffering and then, being moved with compassion, stretched forth His hand and touched them. He never told them beforehand what He was going to do. His laying-on-of-hands was a natural expression of the deep compassion that welled up within Him. It conveyed His self-chosen identification with man in his sufferings and it also conveyed the power of His victory over all evil. His spontaneous touch was an act of atonement. It brought together perfect God and imperfect man.

Many years ago I was haunted by a persistent question for quite a long while. It was, "Are we doing enough?" Much earlier I had felt it was not enough simply to pray for the sick. We ought to pray for the *healing* of the sick, and this I had been doing ever since. Many times, while I prayed for their healing the question "Is this enough?" still persisted. I came to

*Published by Arthur James Ltd., Evesham, Worcs.

realise that Jesus did not send us out with the command to "preach the kingdom and pray for the sick". He told us to *heal* them. Though we were trying to follow in His steps we were not really quite in line with Him. Of course we must pray and pray expectantly for their healing, but this was not quite what Jesus had commissioned us to do. Something vital was being left out. We were throwing the burden back to Him.

This led me on to think of the way we usually give the laying-on-of-hands. With some of us it is spasmodic, with others it has become formalised into some kind of sacred ceremonial, while others, yet again, are afraid to use it at all. They are inhibited by the fear that it might somehow spoil a person's faith if nothing happened. Yet there is no need to fear. If it comes spontaneously out of a movement of Christ's love and compassion burning in us He always blesses it, whatever the results might be. Nor, in such a moment as this, need we worry about whether or not we have a gift. The power and the love are His. All He wants is a willing and trustful channel through whom His healing grace can flow.

Usually we give the laying-on-of-hands by placing both hands upon the sufferer's head and this I was doing. But still the question would not leave me: "Are we doing enough?" For some of those who sought help a further question arose: "But what about those who were suffering from arthritis, for instance, and those with some oft-recurring pain?" Inevitably, the time came when with such sufferers I felt an inner urge compelling me to put my hands on or near the point of pain. For arthritic sufferers in particular—and others as well—I passed my hands first along their shoulders and then gradually down the length of their spines. When I began to obey this urge a new sensitivity developed. Attuning myself to the surrounding presence of the risen Christ and pouring in the loving, healing energies of God abroad in the unseen world about us, I sometimes felt a sensation of heat or of "deadness" in one particular part of the sufferer's spine. Intuitively I kept my hands there for a while.

Without exception as far as I remember, either complete healing has begun or a considerable degree of relief has followed.

Immediately following these ministrations I put my hands on the sufferer's head for a cleansing and healing blessing on his soul, mind and body.

Sometimes, we have to help the sufferer to "claim" the healing that has come to him. After having ministered, for example, to one whose limbs have become locked by arthritis, we take the weight of his arms, each in turn, asking him to see how far he can move them. Again, walking backwards in front of him while holding his hands, we can sometimes enable one who has not walked for years to begin to walk again. There must be no use of force. On the contrary, we encourage a sufferer to be as relaxed as possible so that only the healing power of Christ may flow into every limb.

With Jesus a single command was enough, but for us who stumblingly try to follow in His steps, it is a more laborious process. One day, perhaps, we shall again reach the stage when we can say, "In the name of Jesus, rise up and walk", but we have a long way to go before we can do that.

The principle of helping the sufferer to "claim" his healing was used by Jesus Himself and by the early disciples. Invariably, Jesus would give the sufferer some directive to follow that would set the seal on his healing. There was a man in the synagogue with a withered hand. It was as he obeyed the divine command to stretch it forth that he was healed. There were the lepers who came to Jesus for their healing. It was as they went they were cleansed. At the side of a sick bed Jesus would take the hand of the sufferer and lift her up. Later, following His example, Peter and John, as they commanded the crippled beggar sitting at the Beautiful Gate of the temple to rise and walk, took him by the hand and lifted him up. It was as they did so that his feet and ankle bones received strength.

It is always a great joy and privilege to be asked to minister to sufferers in this way when they have been faithfully upheld in healing prayer by a prayer group. Often my friends in the healing fellowship of Holy Trinity Church, Brompton, London, where many prayer groups are represented at their weekly healing services, feel led to go this one step farther. There are many people on their lists. Sufferers, or friends on their behalf, write for prayer help from all over the world and many wonderful answers have been given to their prayers. Occasionally, however, for some of those they uphold in prayer they get the strong impression that this is not enough. A personal ministration of the laying-on-of-hands is needed. Those of us who have had the privilege of co-operating with these dedicated Christian folk in this way find that the ministration seems to have added power. It rises out of a seed-bed of strong expectant prayer.

All, without exception, can play some part in the church's healing ministry by upholding our sick ones into the presence of Jesus. We can also express our love and concern by caring in practical ways for them. Within the family of the Christian church there is a vast reservoir of healing potential that is never tapped. There are many in every congregation in whom lie gifts waiting to be awakened and developed. They are entrusted to us for God's glory. The pity of it is that we bury them away. These latent potentialities either go to waste or lead those who feel they have them to seek elsewhere for their fulfilment. I sometimes wish that we had an order of lay-healers, similar to our order of lay-readers, in which these gifts could be encouraged, trained and developed.

Thirdly, in Jesus' healing of the man who was deaf and had an impediment in his speech we can see how both medical and sacramental healing are blessed.

Jesus spat and touched his tongue. Saliva, in those days, was commonly thought to have healing properties. It probably has. It is instinctive for an animal to lick its wounds. Our Lord is not averse to using material means of healing. In another place He used clay made of spittle to heal a blind man and when He tells the story of the good Samaritan helping a man who was beaten up He has the Samaritan pouring oil and wine into the wounds. Both were important treatments in the *materia medica* of His day.

Divine healing and medicine are not opposed. Both are working for the same side even though from different planes. Our Western medicine has its origins in the Bible and has largely been developed through the church. The over-zealous Christian who tries to persuade a sufferer that going to a doctor shows lack of faith gets his ideas from somewhere other than the gospel. It certainly does not come from the practice or teaching of our Lord.

Often our hospital chaplains have the privilege of ministering the strong touch of our Lord's healing grace through holy unction (anointing with oil) or the laying-on-of-hands to someone who is receiving or about to receive medical treatment. Such a ministration is not only for the patient's peace of mind or the strengthening of his soul. It also adds divine grace to the treatment and proclaims that all that is done for the patient is sacramental.

In its best and highest sense medical treatment is sacramental. Whether the doctor realises it or not —many of them do—his work is sacred. If he is a committed Christian it becomes a means of grace whereby the treatment is not only valid in its own right but is also a channel, hallowed by his prayer, of the divine love and compassion. A patient who, on his part, responds in faith to this realisation, benefits over and above the value of the treatment he receives.

This great truth is expressed in the sacramental life of the church. Holy unction is a sacrament of healing which gathers into itself all the healing energies of God. It addresses itself not only to the soul of a patient but also to every part of him. And Holy Communion, the central service of the Christian family, focalises into itself the unseen and perfect world of the Kingdom. Through it there flow the fruits of our Lord's victory into every part of our being.

Jesus takes the ordinary things of our life and makes them the channel of the *extra*-ordinary. He takes the natural, and invests it with the super-natural. In His hands the simple, material things become means of grace, channels through which the healing energies of the universe flow.

We have come a long way in the story of the spread of faith in the gentile deanery of Decapolis. It all started with the witness of one man; as it spread it came to express itself in a prayer group and now we come to the end of the story. Let St. Matthew (15, 29-31) recount it to us:

"And Jesus departed from thence (the coasts of Tyre and Sidon, v. 21) and came nigh unto the sea of Galilee; and went up into a mountain, and sat down there.

"And great multitudes came unto him, having with them those that were lame, blind, dumb, maimed, and many others, and cast them down at Jesus' feet; and he healed them:

"Insomuch that the multitude wondered, when they saw the dumb to speak, the maimed to be whole, the lame to walk, and the blind to see:

"And they glorified the God of Israel."

XI

A NEW BEGINNING

HOW CAN WE EVOKE a response of expectant faith today? Jesus did wherever He went. He has not changed and neither have people. Despite all our modern knowledge the capacity for faith is still latent within them. They are looking for, and still ready to respond to, the message of a healing gospel, of One who has authority in the midst of sickness and disease, of a Lord who has overcome the forces of evil. If they cannot hear the message proclaimed by His own body where are they to turn?

We are living in tremendous days. Many of the signs we see about us indicate that we have entered into that final phase of God's unfolding of history to which the prayers and longings of the church have been directed since the day the Lord ascended into heaven. While the bride is being prepared for the coming of the Bridegroom we can be sure that evil forces will come more and more into the open. Before us lies a dividing of the ways and we look into the future with a strange mixture of joy and fear.

I sometimes think we are picking up again where we left off in the pre-Constantine era. Until the great emperor's conversion at the beginning of the fourth century the early church went forward in the power of the Spirit. She overcame the world's hostility and persecution by her inspired obedience to the Lord's command to proclaim to all men everywhere the good news of His victory through the twin avenues of preaching and healing. In those first three centuries the church was the family of a Christ who was risen and ascended yet was still among them. The church was obedient to the guiding of the Spirit. She took risks wherever He led. Caution and mental reservations were not in the vocabulary of those early Christians, against whom even the gates of hell could not prevail.

But the spearhead of their attack against the forces of evil became blunted when, as a result of his conversion, Constantine decreed that Christianity should be the official religion of the Roman Empire. The Christian family became respectable and her leaders regarded as people concerned as much with the new establishment as apostles of a new order. So, for centuries, as a church we put the work of healing on one side and accepted instead the Graeco-Roman ideas about bearing suffering nobly. We became the chaplaincy service to a society we thought would go on forever and devoted ourselves to the creation and preservation of the vast, structured church we have come to know.

Now, after all these centuries, great changes are taking place. We are experiencing the fulfilment of our Lord's prophecy that when the gospel had been proclaimed to all the nations the end-time would begin. By the end of the nineteenth century, a time of great missionary expansion, this task had just about been accomplished. Certainly, we are experiencing a new outpouring of the Holy Spirit wherein all that we have come to understand about the shape and meaning of the church is being dramatically transformed. We are being re-made into the family of God; the gospel that is being restored to us is more akin to that proclaimed by the early church than we have known at any time during the intervening centuries. All this is a happening of the Holy Spirit. It is not of our devising.

This movement is worldwide and every denomination of the Christian church is being touched by its cleansing and renewing power. Much of my work in conducting teaching and healing missions takes me into many countries, and wherever I go I see this same movement of the Holy Spirit. I do not organise my programme. It is shaped for me by the invitations that come through the post. Many, but by no means all, are initially from Anglican sources, but I generally find that other churches in the same area are involved. Anglican and Free, Catholic and Protestant, all are caught up in the movement towards a family in Christ committed to the proclaiming of a gospel of which the healing aspect is an integral part.

Though many individual congregations have not yet been affected by it, those that have find surprising things happening. I am thinking not so much of the healings that begin to take place as of the effect it has on them. The depth of a new dimension enters into their thinking and they become more conscious of the unseen world of Christ's glory and perfection. A joy that was not there before becomes the keynote of their fellowship, a new spirit of expectancy enters into their prayers, and praise becomes their worship's dominant theme. He that was dead is become alive again.

Clergy tell me of the effect it has had on them. It is invariably the same story. When they first embraced the healing ministry they were afraid they might only be adding yet one more concern to all their other commitments; but they came to realise they had done something much more fundamental than that. They were incorporating into their ministry a quality of understanding that it hadn't had before. Often they admit that they have had to re-think their entire theology.

One was a minister who took part with me in a service of healing and saw a woman in his congregation being set free from the trouble he had helped her to accept "for Christ's sake". The gospel that he preaches now has a new depth and a fresh vitality.

Much is being said today about the gifts of the Spirit, of which that of healing is one. For this we have largely to thank the charismatic movement which, like the healing movement, is born of this new age of the Spirit. The charismatic speaks of God's free grace. A gift—or charisma—cannot be earned, neither can it be achieved by any human or psychic means. James Moore Hickson and those other pioneers who worked so hard for the recovery of the healing ministry early in this century often used this word. "The gift of healing is charismatic," Mr. Hickson wrote in 1908, "it is given by God for the enrichment and healing of humanity." In this he was echoing what St. Paul taught when he said, "By grace are ye saved (made whole)."

For my own part I see the charismatic element as being not something apart and distinct from the sacramental but as the vital and essential heart of it. It is in the midst of the sacramental life of the church that the charismatic element finds its true fulfilment and its rightful home. For the charismatic can supply that which sometimes has been lacking in the sacramental. It fills the outward form with Spirit and with life. Sometimes I come upon a church whose worship has gone dead, where the spark has almost become extinguished, where people go more from a sense of duty than with an expectant joy. The form is there but not the power. I have seen such a church completely transformed by the infilling of the Holy Spirit.

In my travels overseas the charismatics with whom I feel most at home are the Catholics in Europe. They have always enjoyed a disciplined life but sometimes perhaps the joy that ought to have been felt in their times of worship and in the saying of the daily offices has been sadly lacking. It is coming back now. There is a thrilling charismatic movement taking place, especially in some of the religious communities. In these churches and communities I have seen the remarkable difference this movement has made to the offering of worship and praise in their Eucharist, the Mass.

I have always believed that the laying-on-of-hands in our confirmation services is really for the baptism of the Spirit. Yet sadly, very sadly, I have sometimes heard a bishop warning his candidates not to expect anything extraordinary to happen to them in that wonderful moment. I still chuckle when I remember the sermon at my own confirmation, though it made me angry at the time. It was by the late Bishop Barnes of Birmingham. He told us that we were descended from monkeys! Many of us who listened to this not new utterance happened to be at university and a few, like myself, were medical students who had only a little while previously completed our studies on the various theories of evolution! We were not very inspired.

A sacrament consists of two parts, the inward and the outward, the visible and the invisible. I think of a sacrament as being like a letter conveying a message, or a vehicle carrying a person, so that a liturgy conveys our worship and a piece of broken bread the very life of our Lord. So, if the laying-on-of-hands in confirmation does not convey the energies of the Holy Spirit, what is it all about?

It is within the context of the sacramental life of the church and against the background of what we mean by the body of Christ or the family of God that I personally see most significance in the renewal of the charismatic element. I believe that an individual Christian receives a charisma, be it of healing or of something else, not as an isolated person but as a member of the congregation to which he belongs. Gifts of the Spirit are meant to bring glory to Christ in that congregation's worship and witness. Where a congregation exists that has an environment of faith in the power of the risen Christ and is filled with a consciousness of the unseen world of the Kingdom, then the channels through which the Holy Spirit can pour His gifts into its members are open. Then, through awareness and obedience, they begin to grow and develop, bringing to the Lord of the church the honour that is due to Him. "To him that hath shall be given, and from him that hath not shall be taken away even that which he hath."

When I read St. Paul's teaching about the gifts of the Spirit in 1 Corinthians 12 and 13 I find myself envisaging a local church so filled with the Holy Spirit that His gifts burst out through its members as blossoms burst from buds on a tree.

I have found such churches coming into being in various parts of the world. Where they were dead or dying they are coming alive again. I think, for example, of St. Paul's Church in Auckland. Like St. Stephen's in Philadelphia, it was about to be declared redundant when Archdeacon Kenneth Prebble undertook to take it over for awhile before a final decision was made. It is a huge, cathedral-sized church in a down-town area surrounded by shops and factories. The congregation for which it was originally built has long since dispersed into the suburbs. No one would have expected anyone to go there now. At least, not until it began its recent new lease of life.

What struck me was the large number of young people taking an active part in the church's life. Every Monday evening there is a service of healing but no one knows what its exact pattern will be. There is a time of fellowship first when they share with one another what the Lord has done for them and what He is leading them to do for others. Out of this fellowship emerge praise and prayer. The strong guiding of the Spirit in the shaping of the service from then onwards is there.

Archdeacon Prebble is a High-churchman. Though he is a loyal Anglican he is Catholic in outlook. Under his leadership a new family in Christ is developing at St. Paul's. I had the privilege of leading a teaching-and-healing mission there and I will never forget the closing service of healing when the huge church was packed to the doors, with people standing at the sides. Some twenty of us, including two doctors, ministered the laying-on-of-hands to most of those who came. After the service one young clergyman, who had been in the congregation, told me that he had shared with others in "seeing" what appeared to be a dove above the heads of the ministrants from which went out concentric circles of light. He felt that what had happened in that church that night would spread beyond its walls to touch the lives of many in New Zealand and beyond.

Memories come of similar services where there has been a strong moving of the Holy Spirit. I think of a church in the Mariendorf area of Berlin where, within the Iron Curtain's grey walls, another packed church experiences the free moving of the Spirit and the healing and releasing touch of the risen Christ. I think of the Catholic College at Koenigstein where, at conferences organised by the German Churches' Healing Movement (Arbeitskreis für biblischen Dienst am Kranken), Christians of all denominations accept the healing ministration of Catholics and Protestants alike. I think, also, of churches in Sweden, Holland, Ireland and Britain, and many other countries where the renewing power of the Holy Spirit is to be felt and seen today.

I shall always remember with great joy the healing service which concluded a mission in the Presbyterian church of Richmond, Virginia. Many hundreds attended and all went forward into the sanctuary to receive the laying-on-of-hands. As they swarmed the central aisle awaiting their turn to kneel before the pastors and elders who ministered to them, many spoke afterwards of a "pool of heavenly light" flooding the area. I know that we were all caught up in a mighty movement of the Holy Spirit sweeping through the church and that everybody present felt His blessing upon them. And I shall always remember the little group of about a dozen young people who sang to us, with the accompaniment of guitars, about the love they had for Jesus. Every one of them radiated the kind of joy that only heaven can give.

This was a church that had been brought alive by

the charismatic movement. Not that any of them mentioned it. They just saw it, experienced it and marvelled. The wonderful thing about that congregation was not so much the gifts of the Spirit that were felt, though they were there, but the fruit.

XII

SO SEND I YOU

AS WE GO OUT with the message of salvation-wholeness we do so conscious of the fact that the victory over evil has already been won and that we are called to take its fruits into all the world. All of us, as members of the body of Christ, are concerned in this. As a clergyman friend wrote, following his first service of healing, "It was not just a re-enactment of the Capernaum scene . . . It didn't matter whether we were in wheel-chairs or apparently fit, we were all in the fight together."

There are two matters we have not so far considered. They have to do with our outgoing work. The first is concerned with preparedness and the second with our weakness and our strength.

It is sometimes suggested that we have to prepare those who are seeking healing before we can minister to them. I never quite know what this means and, I must confess, the thought of it depresses me. Nowhere in the gospels can I find any ground for the suggestion. Jesus always met people at the point of their need. He never insisted on their having the right thoughts and the right approach, whatever those might be. He met them just where they were. If they were moved to seek His help, it was enough.

Whether or not it be in a private interview or before a public service of healing it would be presumptuous of us to impose any preconceived ideas of our own about what should be done before the Lord can heal. It seems to me to be foolish and even dangerous to suggest to a sufferer, if only implicitly, that by correctly following some particular formula he will receive healing. This way only invites "failures".

What disturbs me most is the underlying attitude. It throws the onus of faith on to those to whom we are sent. To take a man by the shoulders saying "You must have faith" is about as helpful as to tell him to lift himself up by his own shoe-strings. To do this is more a judgement on us than on him. As we have seen, although Jesus looks for faith He does so as a matter of response to what He is and to what He preaches. He himself always takes the initiative. To us He says, "Freely ye have received, freely give."

If the quality of our life is such that the world can see Jesus in us as He is, then we can be sure that His promise "I, if I be lifted up, will draw all men unto me" will be fulfilled.

When we turn to the gospels we find that if there is need for preparation it is expected not so much from the sufferer as from the Christian helper. There was one particular moment in our Lord's ministry when this was made quite plain. Jesus had been up into the mountain of transfiguration, leaving nine of his disciples behind. Returning to the scene he was met with utter confusion. There was an epileptic boy there and the nine were powerless to help him. "O faithless generation," Jesus called out, "how long shall I be with you? How long shall I suffer you?" It was to His own disciples as much as to anyone else there that this passionate outburst was addressed.

Later, they asked Him privately why it was they had

been unable to help the boy. He told them, "This kind can come forth by nothing but by prayer (and fasting)."

The onus of preparation, like the onus of faith, is laid by Jesus on the disciples themselves and on all who would follow in His steps. It is the spirit of preparedness that fills the helper before he begins a private interview, the spirit that enters into the vestry before the service begins, that really matters. Jesus spent long nights in prayer. Even He realised the need to be continuously replenished.

When, many years ago, I helped the late Godfrey Mowatt in the monthly services of healing at St. Martin-in-the-Fields, he always insisted that we arrived early. He took no notice if I said we had plenty of time. I soon learned why. After he had put his robes on he would sit quietly in a chair and there begin to enter into the unseen world of the living Christ. I remember how in a little while the power of the divine presence used to fill that little room tucked away in the north-east corner of the building. We were all affected by it. Godfrey's breathing became deep and full as though he were taking in great draughts of the Holy Spirit. Though he was blind he always seemed to know when it was time for the service to begin. Suddenly he would stand and say, "There is great power in this church today. Let us go in."

In those days I learned where the onus of preparation really lay. I learned, too, that during the preparation the whole service from beginning to end had been blessed even before the opening hymn had been announced. What followed in the course of the next hour or so was the unfolding of a pattern that had already been shaped in heaven.

Let us now touch briefly upon our weakness and our strength. Jesus never promised those who work for the coming of His Kingdom a kind of divine protection from the wounds of this world. Indeed, He taught them all the more to expect them. They would know tribulation as He did. Wherever there is a spearhead of the Kingdom it attracts the opposing forces of evil.

This is certainly true of a church or community that embraces healing in its gospel. It is common experience for the devil to make his attacks before or after a healing mission. It is true, too, for individuals. I think of some who were pioneers in the healing movement, men and women whose friendship and trust I valued deeply. While exercising an inspired ministry they yet knew suffering in their own lives. They experienced both kinds: physical and spiritual. The latter might be called a suffering for righteousness' sake. But they never opted out of their calling. It did not inhibit them in their beliefs or in their work. It made them better channels still.

One thing the ministry of healing does to those engaged in it is to make them more sensitive. It is a faculty that is born inevitably from listening to the sad stories of those who come to them for help and from entering empathetically into their sufferings. I know some who experience physical pain before and during ministration. It is a sharing with Christ in the meaning of His incarnation. In divesting Himself of the powers of the Godhead, He became vulnerable to the world's pain.

As we are caught up in this ministry we find ourselves more and more exposed to the hidden forces in the unseen world. We know the happiness of the angels but also the thrusts of the destroyer. I do not think we can have the joys of heaven without, at the same time, knowing something of the desolation of hell. They are like two sides of the same coin. The more we are drawn into the unseen world, the more we become vulnerable to all its powers.

St. Paul spoke of a state of ecstasy into which he had been raised and of having been brought low by a "thorn in the flesh". We do not really know exactly what is meant by this phrase. Usually it means some form of persecution. St. Paul had to suffer plenty of that! But there is always the possibility that some physical trouble suddenly came to him. Often he was accompanied by his doctor, St. Luke.

My own guess, if this is so, is that it was herpes zoster of the fifth cranial nerve (shingles in the head). Those who have suffered from it will know how descriptive this phrase, "thorn in the flesh", is. As the virus works its way along the sensory nerve strands from their roots to the surface it causes a sensation like myriads of tiny thorns in the flesh beneath the surface of the skin, and this can persist intermittently for many years. Without the medical care that our doctors can give today, blindness in one eye easily results. St. Paul's sight was obviously very poor and we know there was something unattractive about his facial appearance.

But whatever it was, it never made him change his mind about healing. He recognised the "thorn in the flesh" as being sent not by God but by Satan. However hurt and buffeted he may have felt he still continued to be a channel through whom the healing power of Christ's Kingdom could flow.

It is strange and even wonderful that out of our sufferings a richer and more powerful stream of healing grace seems to flow into those who seek our help. Sometimes, feeling weak and empty, we are called to minister to someone whose suffering seems, indeed, no worse than ours. As we do so, in simple obedience to the Lord's command, we discover that He blesses the ministration with a greater power.

We can have no doubt that St. Paul experienced this phenomenon in his great ministry to the gentiles and that he came, thereby, to accept his own weakness as a blessed gift. It brought home to him the truth we all have to learn, namely that the power to heal is God's alone. It is no use our spending much time in praying for the gifts of healing, however well intentioned our prayer might be. Were it to be answered we might well find that the gifts we possessed served only to block the flow of God's free grace.

Three times St. Paul prayed for his "thorn" to be removed and three times back came the answer, "My grace is sufficient for thee." It is only when we know we have nothing that we find we have everything. It is only when we are weak that we are strong.

It was not so long afterwards that St. Paul, in writing to the Galatians, was able to say, "I live, yet no longer I, but Christ lives in me." Perhaps that phrase, more than any other in his writings, describes the path along which true healing is to be found. It also indicates the goal at which we should always be aiming if we are really to follow in His healing steps.